TOUCHED BY GOD

D0653240

DIEGO ARMANDO
MARADONA
AND DANIEL ARCUCCI

TOUCHED BY GOD
HOW WE WON THE
MEXICO '86
WORLD CUP

Preface by Víctor Hugo Morales
Translated by Jane Brodie and Wendy Gosselin

Constable • London

CONSTABLE

Originally published in Spanish under the title *Mexico 86: Asi ganamos la copa* by
Sudamericana, an imprint of Penguin Random House Group Editorial S.A., Buenos Aires

First published in the USA in 2017 by Penguin Books, an
imprint of Penguin Random House LLC

First published in Great Britain in 2017 by Constable

1 3 5 7 9 10 8 6 4 2

Copyright © Diego Armando Maradona, 2016
Copyright © Penguin Random House Group Editorial S.A., 2016
Translation copyright © Penguin Random House LLC, 2017

The moral right of the author has been asserted.

All rights reserved.
No part of this publication may be reproduced, stored in a retrieval system,
or transmitted, in any form, or by any means, without the prior permission in
writing of the publisher, nor be otherwise circulated in any form of binding or
cover other than that in which it is published and without a similar condition
including this condition being imposed on the subsequent purchaser.

A CIP catalogue record for this book
is available from the British Library.

ISBN: 978-1-47212-502-6 (hardback)
ISBN: 978-1-47212-503-3 (trade paperback)

Set in Chronicle Text G2
Designed by Sabrina Bowers
Printed and bound in Great Britain by Clays Ltd, St Ives plc

Papers used by Constable are from well-managed forests and other responsible sources.

Constable
An imprint of
Little, Brown Book Group
Carmelite House
50 Victoria Embankment
London EC4Y 0DZ

An Hachette UK Company
www.hachette.co.uk

www.littlebrown.co.uk

Contents

LANCASHIRE COUNTY LIBRARY	
3011813572420 5	
Askews & Holts	09-Jun-2017
796.334092 MAR	£20.00
SWP	

Preface

I Love the Way Diego Describes That Goal

There was a spark in the air as Maradona prepared to redeem his country and take revenge against England. Watching this space alien in an Argentine jersey do the most astounding thing ever done in the history of soccer was like watching a flying saucer burn its way across the sky.

From up near the top of the stadium, you could see some sort of trench, a ditch, and a shining light ripping through, racing like a comet. Far below in the shadows, in the bowl-shaped Azteca stadium, something happened—Maradona did something that usually occurs only up in the heavens. Like a shooting star tearing a hole in the dark sky, Diego rushed by, as proud as a flag bearer leading his army into a critical battle. Then he darted past the English flanks, leaping over legs as he attempted the impossible. And, like a mountain climber, he planted his flag at the peak.

Jorge Valdano, who was right behind him that day, once said that Diego apologized to him for not passing him the ball. Diego said he just didn't get the chance. Valdano and the other players wondered how he could possibly have been thinking about that during his unforgettable run.

From one of the press boxes in the stadium—I was working as a sports commentator—I shouted that Diego had just made "the greatest play of all time," and then I added a phrase that would be repeated endlessly, calling Diego "the cosmic kite." I went on to work in sports journalism for some thirty years, but that broadcast is what everyone remembers: my entire career has been wrapped up in Diego's still unsurpassed play.

How many plays are possible in the heat of the match? What did Diego, an artist at the game, see on the field? He made a series of intentional mistakes from the time he got the ball until he reached the goalpost. Sandwiched between hundreds of other commentators, I was forced to abandon all the conventions of my trade by the visions of everything he was doing and everything he might have done.

"Genius, genius, genius," was the modest word I repeated as the fearless player approached the summit, plowing through the furrow he was making on the turf. At what point did Maradona decide to go for the goal? As he moved forward, he kept his eye on the ball, but how many legs, how many square feet of land came into his peripheral vision? He was able to connect with the ball, to stop, to start up again at an angle, to finish up the play from afar. In a thousand different ways, this play was one in a billion.

Courage, intuition, and "a god behind God," as Jorge Luis Borges would have said, made this a unique play for all times. By the time the English team's sense of powerlessness and disbelief had passed, Maradona had placed the ball deep inside the net.

"I want to cry," is what I said, my hand curled into a fist, my body wrapped up in cables, leaning over my desk as Maradona ran off the field to celebrate his feat.

His entire body was shaking as he let out a cry of joy, and his mind went blank, as if a cloud had exploded behind his closed eyes. It's wasn't just any goal. Emotions built up over several years poured into the sieve of reason. It was Diego's feat, the triumph of the one so beloved to soccer fans. It meant that Argentina had made it to the World Cup semifinals.

It was a goal against the English, and hundreds of young men who should have been shouting in joy were absent: their voices had been silenced four years earlier in the cold of the Malvinas (the Falkland Islands). It took place at a rival's stadium. And it was the most beautiful and the boldest, the most courageous and inventive play that soccer had ever produced.

Thirty years later, the man himself cannot erase its mark. He jumps farther, runs faster, has more endurance than the rest: the universe itself may expand into infinity, but it can't outrun Maradona. It's no small feat. You have to take control of the ball on your side of the field, dodge any rival who gets in your way, face the goalie, and then knock the ball into the net. And it has to be at the World Cup.

And, speaking of Borges, in the short story "The Library of Babel" he imagines every possible book, just as that day Diego wrote everything that could ever be written about soccer, the sport he took to a whole new level.

In a single play, he wrote the book on intuition, on boldness and skill, the book on courage, strength, cunning, genius, memory, and everything else found in the soccer library.

When, at the beginning of the match, the players formed two lines, Diego egged on his fellow teammates. They remember how their captain told them exactly what their rivals would do that day. The words he used were anything but formal. They came from the book of the potrero, with all the challenges it holds. With the insolence of a man who doesn't seem at all worried about the rules of the game even though the survival of the entire group is at stake, he encouraged them to be intrepid, to leap into the void, even if that meant falling to their death. He couldn't have known at that point that the same mixture of mischief and art he used in his words to his teammates would be what he deployed in the decisive play of the most exciting match in Argentine history. If he had said, "We'll beat them, no matter what it takes," then the goal he knocked in with his hand would have made sense. If he had said something about showing what Argentina knew about soccer, there would not have been any need for further explanation: "the goal against the English" would have sufficed. His fellow players cannot remember a single word he said. Or maybe they are just too proud. But they all say that Diego talked their ears off.

I love the way Diego describes that goal and that match. The '86 World Cup saw the culmination of a genius who understood just what a world championship means to history. And this epic tale tells still more about his greatness. You couldn't write this myth off as one of life's mysteries. Maradona was aware of the challenge that lay before him. It was a duel he had foreseen. To be or not to be, with the whole world watching. He still had to fashion the fame that was not yet wholly his own. He readied himself like Rocky Balboa, offering his body in a sacrifice that would be in vain unless he brought the cup home with him. That's how cruel life is when you're the runner-up. The close-up of him bolting toward the goal in the match against Italy shows just how far he had come in his aspiration to be the very best. It can be seen in the way he goes past the mark, like a sprinter running the last fifteen feet. It can be seen in the perfect leap to hit the ball in the air, not waiting for it to come down to his foot—in the artistic grace he used to define the play.

Everything is easier when there are no expectations. Few can bear the weight of the hopes of millions, watching with bated breath as the dreaded encounter unfolds. But Diego knew he would be bringing the World Cup home. Rather than the weight of dread, what he carried on his shoulders was the promise of a newly democratic country that needed to show it could now be a champion. That was the real goal, and, if he failed, the only one who would have to give explanations would be Diego himself.

When it came to standing up for others, Diego was always there. He never lost his rebel spirit or turned his back on his past. His class consciousness did not waver, no matter how many castles welcomed him or royalty courted him. He was still, first and foremost, a soccer player, and darkness falls over the potrero as the sun goes down, like a postcard from a dream.

Yet if we listen to his story, we can discover more about what it means to be Maradona. I believe readers will enjoy learning about parts of his life that, until now, have gone untold. Diego in front of the mirror: his story, his life, his teammates, his coaches, as well as adversaries, stadiums, goalies. Finally face-to-face with the judge, the question he seems to ask is, "What else do they want from me?"

It might be hard for Diego to explain what about him, exactly, made his television special, *De Zurda*, so wildly popular across Latin American during the 2014 World Cup in Brazil.

Telesur was not allowed to rebroadcast the goals or the key plays from the matches, but Maradona's magic was more than enough for viewers. Thanks to the program's guest stars and his smiling face and ongoing battles against corruption in the FIFA, Maradona was able to establish a rapport with viewers across the continent—regardless of the many problems he faced.

On that program, up close, it suddenly became clear how hard it is to be Maradona, the man who, though just a few feet away from the world's best beaches, was not allowed to set foot on them. Despite tremendous demands, he was always cordial to the television crew. Diego's respect, manners, and generosity won over the few dozen Argentines and Venezuelans on the TV crew. Endlessly riddled by controversy, Diego never lost patience with anyone during the long month that the program lasted. He knew—as he had known when he went out on the field—that this was his team. On the last night of the program's filming, the whole TV crew—many of whom had met many big stars during years of work behind the cameras—offered Diego a show of their friendship and gratitude, an unforgettable memento of those weeks together.

Diego was always willing to listen to the suggestions of crew members and directors. He would predict the outcome of corner kicks at barbecues and, to the shock of the goalies, the ball would go in exactly as he had called it. For these reasons and so many more, Diego continued to win the affection of everyone fortunate enough to spend time with him.

Because it was there, working at his side, that Diego became something more than the man who walked onto the field with the English at the start of a match like none other, saying,

"You know we can't lose this one—right, guys? We have to give our lives for those who gave their lives over there, you know where. Here it's eleven against eleven, and we're going to trample them, got it?" And off he went, a flag in one hand and a whole country behind him.

VÍCTOR HUGO MORALES

Introduction

I Wasn't So Crazy After All, Now Was I?

This is Diego Armando Maradona speaking, the man who scored two goals against England and one of the few Argentines who knows how much the World Cup actually weighs.

I don't know why, but last Christmas, the first one the whole family spent together at the old house in Villa Devoto, in Buenos Aires—everyone except for doña Tota and don Diego, my beloved mom and dad, that is—that phrase came to me. It's not the first time a line has come to me like that. The same thing happened when I said, "The ball doesn't stain," on the day of the tribute match at the Bombonera, the Boca Juniors club's home stadium. Many still believe that someone writes those phrases for me. But that's not true. They come straight up from the heart to my head. That Christmas Eve, I looked up at the sky and thanked my folks for everything they had given me in life—which was a lot, much more than I have given them. They gave me everything, absolutely everything, they had. And they were always at my side, in good times and in bad. And, let me tell you, there have been some bad times...

That Christmas Eve, someone—I can't remember who—gave me a replica of the World Cup. And when I held the golden trophy in my hands again, when I rocked it in my arms like a baby, I realized that almost thirty years had gone by since that day in Mexico when I had held the real cup. And I also realized that the joy my folks felt on that day so many years ago must have been one of the best gifts I ever gave them. The best one. It was a gift for them and for all Argentines. The ones who were behind us . . . and the ones who weren't. Because, in the end, the people—all of them—took to the streets to celebrate.

And I also realized that the more time goes by, the heavier the cup gets. Three decades later, those ten-odd pounds feel like a ton. Let me make one thing perfectly clear: I am in no way pleased that no other Argentine player has lifted the cup since 1986. If I were, I'd be a traitor. Just as I'd be a traitor if I didn't share every last thing we went through back then, tell it the way it comes out, the way I lived it. Because that's the way I talk—that's the way Maradona talks. As I'll say again and again in the coming pages, my body took plenty of blows over the years, but my memory is intact.

I admit it: there are some things I see differently thirty years later. I think I have a right to that. I've changed a lot, it's true, and many speak of my inner contradictions. But there's one thing that hasn't changed, one point where I've never contradicted myself: when I take on a cause, I do so whole-heartedly. That's why I can say today—so many years later—that I would have liked Bilardo to do for me what I did for him when push came to shove. That's all. For him to have gone out on a limb for me the way I did for him. Because he knows better than anyone how I put myself out there for him when the Menotti and Bilardo camps were at war. I fought for a cause that should have been everyone's. I put the Argentine jersey above my personal preferences, and even though I had a special place in my heart for Menotti, I never admitted that in public.

The rest is history. You remember it the best you can; you remember it how you feel it. That's why I say that this is *my* truth. Everyone has his own.

The one thing I would shout for all to hear and write for all to read—something that I myself can't forget—is that everyone acted like I was crazy when I said we were going to win it. I wasn't so crazy after all, now was I? In the end, we did win, we won it all.

And on these pages, I'm going to tell how we did it.

Many ask me about that celebrated thing I said when, still just a Cebollita (I played for the Argentinos Juniors team), a group of us caught the attention of Francis Cornejo, the coach. You know the tape—it's been on TV so many times. I was on television in black and white—more black than white, in my case—saying, "My greatest dream is to play in the World Cup. My second greatest is to win." I hadn't finished yet, but someone cut me off there and everyone thought I was talking about winning the World Cup. What I was really talking about, though, was winning the minor-league tournament with my teammates, my friends! The video came out in its entirety not long ago. For me, the minor league was like the national all-star team. But there was no way I was going to be talking about winning the World Cup. I didn't even have a television set back them. That must have been before the '74 World Cup. I was totally clueless . . . But that's how it goes.

How could I possibly have imagined that I would end up somewhere like Dubai, describing what we did in Mexico thirty years ago? In Dubai! From Villa Fiorito to Dubai, that's where my life has taken me. And I am so grateful to these people, who took me in when my own country turned its back on me. They have given me a job, love, and even money. But, mostly, I have gotten used to them and not the other way around. They gave me peace of mind when I needed it most, because I was tormented by what had happened in 2010 after the World Cup in South Africa.

I like sitting here in front of one of the many television sets I have in my house in Palm Jumeirah and watching games played everywhere on earth, from Italy to England. I watch everything. And now I sit down to watch the matches from the '86 World Cup in Mexico once again.

Believe it or not, I hadn't ever actually seen them.

Of course I had watched the goals against England thousands of times (they are on TV all the time). But I hadn't seen the other games until now. And when I watch them play-by-play, so many years later, I go through it all again: I feel the pain of the South Koreans' kicks and the suspense of the duel with the Italians; I am once again annoyed by the Bulgarians and captivated by the magic spell I cast on the Uruguayans; I see how I took flight in the match against the Belgians and celebrated when we beat the Germans. As I watch it all again, a flood of memories pours over me.

My memories. Everyone remembers it the way they want to. This is how I remember it. I remember getting ready to take flight. And that's exactly what I did. I played fair even though they played dirty. Drugs made me a worse player, not a better one. Do you have any idea the player I would have been if it weren't for the drugs? I would have been that player you saw in Mexico, for years on end. That was the happiest I have ever been on the soccer field.

There, in Mexico, my hunger to win the World Cup took precedence over anything and everything else. I put aside my spot in Napoli and my own personal preferences as a player; I let my family know that this was my chance. I spoke to my teammates for hours on end so that we were all on the same wavelength. That is the message I want to convey to Messi, and to all the Messis who—I hope—will follow.

When they asked me what we were there for, once we were all focused and had started training the way I wanted us to, I said, "To be the world champions." And when they asked me what I was there for, I said, "To prove that I'm the best in the world." I wasn't being a big shot, not at all. I was just confident and I wanted to convey that to the rest of the team. Didn't they believe in us? Didn't they believe in me? Look out, because we did believe. I did believe. Crazy Maradona believed.

When they asked Platini the same question, he said, "I don't know—there's the altitude issue." When they asked Zico, he said, "I'm not sure—my knee is injured and the team has to come together." Same thing when they asked Rummenigge. Those were our rivals, my rivals.

People may say a lot of things about me, but one thing's for sure: when I set my mind to something, I get it. And with my eye on the ball, I was always sure I would be able to get whatever I set my mind to. Valdano used to say to me that when I touched the ball, it was like I was making love to it. And there was something to that . . .

Was I scared? Of course I was! When there are a lot of people waiting to see if you can make a dream come true, you're scared. How could you not be?

At those moments—and there were a few of them in the World Cup that year, before the final—I would think of Tota, my mom. And I would say—and I mean say out loud, not to myself—"I'm scared shitless, Tota. Come help me, please." But there was no way Tota was going to come, because she was in Buenos Aires. I had asked them all to stay behind, except for my dad, because I wanted to stay 100 percent focused on the game. On playing and winning. That was what made me happy.

I was just a kid. And I still am. I remember that I dedicated that World Cup to all the kids around the world. I did—you can look it up. It was the first thing I said at the press conference at Azteca stadium when they asked me who it was for. "It's for all the kids around the world," I said, and I blew them a kiss.

Before that, before celebrating with the rest of the team, I had gotten together with Carmando, Salvatore Carmando, a masseuse from Naples, whom I had taken to Mexico with me. He gave me a kiss on the forehead and said, "Diego, you're the champion of the world, the greatest . . . Do you have any idea what that means?" "No," I said. "All I know is that I am the happiest man in the world."

Many, many years later—thirty, in fact—I finally understood that being happy means making others happy. And I think that Argentines were happy about what we did in Mexico. I may have screwed up plenty in my day—I did: there's no doubt about it—but nobody anywhere is ever going to forget those two goals I scored against the English, with the wound of the Malvinas still open. I lifted up that World Cup—something no other Argentine has done since.

Nobody is ever going to forget that. Least of all me.

But, just in case, I'm going to tell it again. I'll tell it my way, which will certainly be different from the way others have told it. And that is why I say and write again and again: this is Diego Armando Maradona speaking, the man who scored two goals against the English—and one of the few Argentines who knows how much the World Cup weighs.

TOUCHED BY GOD

CHAPTER 1

The Team Nobody Wanted

Soon before the World Cup—it must have been April '86—the country was facing problems even more serious than the national team. But that's the way we Argentines were, and it's the way we still are. Politics has always meddled in soccer; it has always used soccer to its own ends. And, unfortunately, that's not going to change. Back then, the president, Raúl Alfonsín, said he wasn't pleased with how the team was playing, and rumors began to circulate that the government wanted to get rid of the coach, Carlos Bilardo. In fact, Rodolfo O'Reilly, who—along with Osvaldo Otero—worked with the government at the Recreation and Sports Department, called me up to tell me that they were going to fire Bilardo.

It was eleven at night in Italy when the phone rang. "That's weird," I thought. They put the call through. The first thing I said was, "I'm sorry, but how did you get this number?"

"The government has everyone's number—didn't you know?"

"Is that so? Well, I've never even set eyes on you, and you think you can call me at home at eleven at night? Do you even

know what time it is here? But I have something more important to say to you . . ."

"I'm so sorry, Diego. What is it you have to say?"

"If you get rid of Bilardo, I'm out the door. So, just to be
perfectly clear, you'd be firing two guys instead of one. If he
goes, I go."

And I hung up.

I want to make this clear here and now: I did not stab Bilardo in the back when the government called me about getting rid of him. He, on the other hand, betrayed me almost
thirty years later.

In those days, I was on César Luis Menotti's side, but I did
everything for the cause, for the team, because I was sure
that we would get somewhere. And the cause had been limp-
ing along, truth be told. I wanted to put an end to everything
that had been done to hurt the team, and that's exactly what
I did. I had decided to take that team to victory, and that's exactly what I did. How about that, Alfonsín?! With all the crap
he had to deal with, what was he doing worrying about Bilardo? Come on.

I did everything for the cause, for the guys, and even for Bilardo. He wasn't a bad guy. And it's without bitterness that I
say that since he went to work for the Asociación de Fútbol Argentino (AFA), after the 2010 World Cup in South Africa, he's
been dead to me. And nobody can bring him back to life in my
eyes. They told me he wanted to talk to me, but there's no way.
And I mean no way. I meant it when I said it, and I mean it even
more today. None of this is overblown. It's the truth, my truth.

Of course, nothing will make me forget how he went all
the way to Barcelona to tell me his vision. But that doesn't
have anything to do with it. And the time has come to tell it

exactly as it happened, our experience on the ground and not just Bilardo's vision.

Carlos didn't let us train! I am always surprised to hear everyone talk about Bilardo's tactics. Come on! I mean, one day before the match against Korea we had no idea what our strategy was. We didn't know if Burruchaga would be on the left side or on the right side, if Sergio Daniel "Checho" Batista would cover midfield or stay on the wing . . .

But—I must admit—it's also true that Bilardo came for me when nobody seemed to remember me. And I mean nobody.

MARADONA WANTED THE REMATCH

Everyone was more worried about Daniel Passarella than about Maradona, and he showed up in Lloret de Mar one day during the offseason. It was March '83, and there was still a chill in the air. But I didn't feel the cold or the heat. All I cared about was training to start playing again. I had been on the bench for almost three months because of the goddamn hepatitis, which I had caught in December of '82. We had done special preseason training with Joan Malgosa, a coach for Barça (Barcelona), and Ricardo Próstamo, who had been a teammate of mine at Argentinos Juniors, had kept me company. It wouldn't be long before—after so many months—I would finally be able to kick a ball around, and I was dying to. I was also anxious because there was talk that the coach, the German Udo Lattek, was on his way out. He had driven us to ground with his workouts, but he never let us near the ball. Rumor had it that César Luis "El Flaco" Menotti would replace him. That was, for me, a blessing. I would finally feel comfortable at Barça. The whole thing was inspiring.

Bilardo showed up out of nowhere with Jorge Cytersz-piler, who was still my representative back then. Night fell and he came straight over from Barajas airport. We talked for a while before dinner, and the next morning the madman asked me for a pair of shorts so we could go jogging together. Almost four miles—the last four in my workout. We jogged, walked, and then jogged again. And we talked. We talked a ton. And I remember exactly what was said:

"I wanted to know how you're doing."

"Just fine. I haven't played for three months, but tomorrow I'm back at the ball, and then there's no stopping me."

"Good. I wanted to talk to you about forming part of the national team."

"Listen, Carlos, my contract says that, in addition to the qualifying rounds, I can play in any match as long as Barcelona doesn't have a major commitment on the same day. But my only major commitment is to the Argentine jersey."

Then he started in about the dough. Bilardo was always talking about bread. "Money" is the word he used for it. He asked if I was going to demand any special compensation.

"No, don't you worry about that . . . You think I have money problems? If I play, it'll be for the team, to defend the Argentine jersey. I couldn't care less about the cash."

I hadn't played in the '78 cup. I did play in '82—but some things had gone wrong, and I was one of them. I was physically exhausted before we even started. But it was not as if that year had been a total disaster. In typical Argentine fashion, when we won it in '78, everything was roses. And in '82, because we lost it, we were all in the doghouse. But that's not fair.

Anyway, I was not at the top of my game. And I wanted a rematch. With all my soul, I wanted one.

In my first interview after returning from the '82 cup, I said I had not blown it, that I had done the best I could. But I knew perfectly well that I was the one who had lost the most that time. So many expectations, so much publicity, so many guys with sticks up their asses waiting to see me go down. And I remember perfectly well saying, "Come on, guys, come to your senses. In Argentina there are a lot of things much more important than Maradona. I want to get that cup out of my mind and start thinking about the next one, about '86." That's what I said in '82. And one year later, I was already training to show that I meant it.

Bilardo started telling me his ideas about how I should play and so forth. He told me not to worry about the hepatitis thing. Letanú and Trobbiani, two of his players on the Estudiantes team, had come down with it. At first it was hard for them to get back into the swing of things, but then everything got back on track. And, in terms of the game, he was willing to let me do whatever I wanted. He wanted me to feel free, to play where I saw fit; the others would come together around me. He wanted me upfield; I shouldn't have to mark another player (like hell I wouldn't) like Karl-Heinz Rummenigge and Hansi Müller on the German team did. He loved West Germany. I remember that he later went to talk to Stielike, who was a sweeper for Madrid. He went to see old man Di Stéfano too. Alfredo's a great guy. I've always loved him. He was a hothead—just like me—and a man ahead of his times. What he told Bilardo back then was that Argentine soccer needed to be flexible and dynamic; everyone had to mark an opponent, not just make their own plays. And he was right, actually.

And then Bilardo said something to me that I will never

forget as long as I live. "And one more thing: you'll be the captain of the team."

My heart caught fire! If I didn't drop dead from a heart attack on the spot, I never will. And to this day, whenever someone tells me that I was, that I am—that I still am!—the captain of the national team, I get the same feeling in my chest. It's just as thrilling as holding your grandson in your arms. You're the one taking command—it's all in your hands. There's nothing greater than being the captain of any team, let alone the national team. You're the man, no two ways about it.

I had the captain's armband of the Argentinos Junior team, of Juvenil, and of Boca—I must have collected some two hundred, since whenever I would travel, I would buy one. But what I wanted was to actually be the captain of the national team. I was only twenty-four years old, but I felt I was ready. Passarella had been captain until then, but now it was my turn.

When they make you captain, you'd better know all the players well. I would have people bring me videos to see how different guys played. I would get my brothers and my nephews on the phone and ask them. They helped me a lot: "That guy knows what he's doing." "That one should pass the ball more." It's funny now, but back then you couldn't just watch a game on TV. You had to get information wherever you could. And I would look for it everywhere. Especially once I became captain.

OF COURSE THAT'S WHAT MARADONA'S TEAM WOULD BE LIKE

As soon as my dream of being the captain of the national team had come true, I made a decision: all the players had to feel that wearing the country's jersey was the most important thing in the world, no matter how much dough you could make playing for a European club.

That was what I wanted Maradona's team to be like. That was what I wanted to establish.

It was also really important to me when Bilardo told me I would always be a starter, which is exactly what I said to Javier Mascherano many years later. I should have done the same thing with Messi—though I never told him that (a piece of unfinished business). I accept those who referred to the national team as "Maradona plus ten," just as I later called it "Mascherano plus ten." But I never thought I could win a game on my own, because that's simply not possible. That's why I thank all my teammates for their sacrifices . . . all of them except Passarella, that is.

But I'm getting way ahead of myself. It was March '83 and the story was just getting started. And almost two years would go by before I put the Argentine national team's jersey back on. Incredible, but true. So much would happen in the meantime. As is always the case with me, one year in my life is like three or four in everyone else's.

I was back on the field one week after that meeting with Bilardo. I had been out with hepatitis for three months. The game against Betis ended in a tie, one to one. But what mattered most was that "El Flaco" Menotti was debuting as the coach. And with El Flaco on board everything was different for everyone. The guys loved him because of how he treated them. I mean, they had had the German coach and Menotti could win you over with his words. Imagine, Guardiola himself went to see El Flaco when he agreed to be the coach. Even today, when those guys get together, the first thing they do is ask about El Flaco.

I really enjoyed playing for that Barcelona team, and I remember great games like the one against Real Madrid at the Bernabéu stadium. We won, two to nothing, and I scored an amazing goal; they still show it on television. I started off from beyond midfield, in a devastating counterattack. The goalie, Augustín, came out of the penalty area. I went past him and there was nothing between me and the goal. I saw that Juan José—a short little defense player with long blond hair and a beard—was coming up from behind. I faked heading straight for the goal, but then I stopped short and waited; when he reached me I pushed the ball left with the outside of my foot, almost right on the goal line. The guy went straight past me and ended up straddling one of the goalposts. Just thinking about it hurts. And then I just flipped the ball into the goal, easy as pie . . . The entire stadium gave me a standing ovation.

Under "El Flaco" Menotti, we finished fourth in the league. I was able to play in the last seven games of the season, and we even won the Copa del Rey, beating Real Madrid under the great don Alfredo Di Stéfano. The idea was to march on to the next tournament.

I thought that nothing as bad as the hepatitis would ever happen to me again. But I was wrong . . . We started out losing, but that wasn't the worst part. The worst part was the fourth game of the season, when Bilbao's Athletic came to play at Camp Nou stadium. It was a classic matchup against the Basques, and the teams really gave it their all.

It sounds like something out of a novel, but it's true. It actually happened to me, and it still hurts.

I've told the story before and I am happy to tell it again because it involves someone who was crucial at that time and would be again once the World Cup was close at hand and there wasn't much time left. I am talking about Dr. Rubén Darío Oliva, "the Doc" or "El Loco," with all due respect. He knows that's what I call him. And I had to call him then— that's right, when the Basque player Goikoetxea broke my leg.

It was September 24, 1983. I remember the date as if I had scored a big goal that day or something. How could I ever forget the worst injury of my entire career!? They would really knock you around in Spanish soccer back then! It was a miracle that someone didn't break a bone every single game. I always tell the story about the kid I went to see in the hospital; he had been run over by a car and he wanted to meet me. When I was leaving his room—in a rush because the match against Bilbao was that day—the kid shouted to me from the hospital bed that I should be careful because they were going to come after me. I remember that shivers ran down my spine—those things freak you out. But, by then, I was used to getting knocked around—why should this game be any different?

The game was going well for us. We were winning, three to nothing, and the German player Schuster was taking care of Goikoetxea. There was some bad blood there because the Basque had injured him before. The stadium was on fire: everyone was backing the German, and Goikoetxea wanted to eat him alive. Since he was marking me, he was right by my side, so I said to him, "Easy does it, Goiko. They're going to give you a warning and you guys are behind, three nothing..."

I swear I was not making fun of him. I really wasn't. I used to talk to the players on the other team that way, especially the ones who were marking me. Naturally, I always kept an eye on how they were treating me. But that night I didn't see it coming. If I had, I would have jumped back.

The play has been shown on TV thousands of times and now you can see it online. I went for the ball in the midfield area, slightly downfield. I toe poked the ball to my left in what they now call "ball control," to spin before taking off—my best move. With a short sprint, I killed the defense.

But as soon as I had brought my left foot down, to spin around before taking off, I felt it. I swear it sounded just like a piece of wood splitting. I can still feel it. The first guy who came up to me, I remember, was Migueli. "Are you all right?" he shouted. "He broke my leg. He broke it," I answered, crying.

They took me to the hospital straight from Camp Nou, in a pathetic little van—unthinkable today. It wasn't even an ambulance. And when I got to the room, the first thing I wanted to know—the only thing—was when I would be able to get back on the field, if I was going to be able to get back on the field. Soon "El Flaco" Menotti came to see me. He leaned over me and with that smoker's voice of his, said, "You'll get better quick, Diego. And let's hope that all this pain is good for something. Let's hope it puts an end to all this violence." I mean, they really played rough back then.

And when Dr. Rafael González-Adrio, the doctor who was going to operate on me, came in, I said to him, "I want to play again soon, Doc. Do whatever you have to do, but I want to play again soon."

But for that to happen, I would need the magic hands. "The Doc," "El Loco." That's right, Oliva. He went to Buenos Aires with me. I called him up, because he lived in Milan. But he came right away. In fact, he had done so on more than one occasion, no matter how trivial what I had may have been. He came for a muscle ache, for mild discomfort. So imagine how he acted now. What's more, if he had made it there that evening, I'm sure they wouldn't have operated on me. No doubt in my mind. With his bare hands, the guy could take care of a broken bone—no need for surgery.

As I said before, I'm telling this story again because that guy was crucial to my performance at the World Cup. That day, he proposed a wager to Dr. González-Adrio.

"If in fifteen days' time the X-ray shows that the bone is beginning to heal, I'll take over the treatment. If not, it's all yours," he said. "But of course," said the Spaniard, who assumed it would be six months before I could put any weight on my leg.

Within fifteen days, I put my ankle in Oliva's wise hands. He took off the cast, took an X-ray, and told me to put my weight on it.

All the fear comes rushing back as I tell the story.

"Are you crazy?" I said.

But I put my weight on it and it didn't hurt.

One week later, we went to see González-Adrio, to do some tests. He almost had a heart attack when he saw me walk in on crutches but with no cast. "Would you mind holding these for me, doc," I asked, handing him my crutches to walk down the stairs.

Oliva won the bet, of course, and I went back to Buenos Aires to recover. In 106 days, I was playing again, against Sevilla. We won, three to nothing, and I scored two goals. "El Flaco" Menotti took me out before the game was over, and I remember getting one of the largest ovations of my career. If you ask me, it was really for Oliva. Thanks to him, my ankle was still my ankle. He actually told me that I played so well partly because my ankle had a larger pivot than most.

Well, it was thanks to his hard work that I could still pivot like that. I was shipshape. That's not the only thing I managed not to lose—but that comes later, closer to the World Cup. I had to move first...

TO NAPOLI AND ANOTHER LIFE

Meanwhile, a whole year had gone by since that first meeting with Bilardo, and I had yet to put on the national team's jersey. And it would be another year before I did. Not once in '84. I mean, when I think about it now I can't believe it. How did I stand it? Not even I know how. Bilardo said he didn't call us because the foreign clubs wouldn't let us play exhibition matches. That's one thing that has changed for the better, right? But if it hadn't, if no one had stood up to the clubs to make them turn over their players despite all the money at stake, there wouldn't be any national teams today. They would be league all-star teams and the most powerful leagues, the ones with the most cash, would have the best players. In fact, something like that had occurred to Silvio Berlusconi when he was the big cheese in Milan and all the great players went to AC Milan. But one thing I can say for sure, I would never have agreed to it. I would never have worn a jersey that wasn't blue and white.

It's true that I changed jerseys at that time, but only from one club to another. I had reached my limit with Barcelona. My relationship with Josep Lluís Núñez, the president of the club, was awful, and I left on terrible terms. I mean, it came to blows. Even with the players for Athletic Bilbao at the other Copa del Rey final.

So I went to Napoli, where I started another life. I landed

in San Paolo stadium in July of '84, during a really rough spell for the national team. But it was an even rougher spell for me. Financially, I was ruined. As I've said before, I had to start all over at that time. Napoli was an opportunity. I was a broken man, and I don't mean just my ankle. I was penniless, and I started again from scratch . . .

.   I say it was one of the worst moments for the national team because they were playing a series of exhibition matches—the ones Bilardo didn't call us for because the clubs wouldn't let us play—and they weren't doing well at all. They tied Brazil, lost and tied against Uruguay, lost to Colombia . . . And that's when the harsh criticism set in. They really laid into the team. I think they were so harsh because they associated Bilardo with Osvaldo Zubeldía. They were biased against Bilardo for having had Zubeldía as his coach, for where he came from, for what had happened, or what they said had happened—who knows?—at the Estudiantes club in La Plata. It was a dispute about style more than anything, but they really went at it. The Menotti camp versus the Bilardo camp, and the other way around—and everything that was behind all that. And we players were caught in the middle.

But soon, in September, when I was beginning to play with Napoli in the tournament, I realized it was not going to be easy, that I was really going to have to give it my all. At that point, the national team stepped up with a great tour in Europe: they beat Switzerland, Belgium, and West Germany. And that day—in Düsseldorf, I think—when it was three to one, with two goals by José Daniel "Bocha" Ponce and one by Jorge "Burru" Burruchaga, plus the shot from midfield by "Bocha" that ended up denting the crossbar. And Bilardo announced publicly once again that I was on the starting lineup.

And Beckenbauer—Franz Beckenbauer, that's right—the coach of the West German national team, who was sitting next to him, butted in, saying, "If you aren't going to put him in, give him to me."

At that point, I was as worried about getting Napoli up to speed as I was about my own financial situation. And I was waiting for the moment when I would be able to play with the national team again. The idea that it wouldn't happen until the qualifying round seemed crazy to me. That was a hundred years away. But anything else would mean going against the rules.

But, you know me. Going against the rules—especially if the rules are unfair—has never been much skin off my back. No skin at all, in fact.

I tried to do my best on the field, leaving no room for doubt that my heart was in it for Napoli. But I wanted to do the same thing for the national team. It was a struggle, but I loved it: I wanted to go for broke no matter what team I was playing for.

I was in constant touch with the guys on the national team. Every time they played, I would send them telegrams, best wishes. I would make statements. I wanted them to know that I was with them, even though I wasn't on the field.

I wanted them to know that I was their captain.

I remember that around that time I got really ticked off at Juan Carlos "Toto" Lorenzo, a guy who was really beloved in Italy and who had a lot of clout there. They asked him about the choice of captain, why it had been me and not Passarella—boy, they loved to talk about Passarella!—and Toto said you had to think about what being a captain means. The most important thing is to be the coach's main ally. The captain has to be the one who takes in all the information in the locker room, a guy trusted by his teammates, someone they can count on for big things—the one who would be accountable when push came to shove. Lorenzo said that Passarella— here we go again with Passarella!—was a leader, a caudillo. He remembered once at Wembley Stadium seeing with his own eyes how Passarella had shown Kevin Keegan who was running the team. And he wondered out loud if I, if Maradona, would be ready to take on all that responsibility. You bet your ass I was! It was the only thing I wanted in the whole world. But I had to get out on the field to show it, to show it all.

Meanwhile, I was keeping an eye on the national team from afar. I saw how Bilardo was putting together the team with the group of players in Argentina: Pumpido, Ruggeri, Garré, Gareca, Camino, Brown, Dertycia, Trossero, Pasculli, Rinaldi, Burruchaga, Russo, Ponce, Giusti, Márcico, Islas, Clausen, Bochini. Those were the guys in preseason play, with an eye to the qualifying rounds. At a certain point, I had to join that group, of course, as did "Pato" Fillol and, naturally, Passarella, because the press was hot for him; they were always asking Bilardo about him. Journalists didn't ask him about me, just him. And the other guys on the team who were playing for foreign clubs would be Valdano, Barbas, Calderón. That's it. It wasn't the way it is now, where most play abroad. Not at all. Back then, it was three or four at the most.

I followed it all from afar, from 3 Via Scipione Capece, my new home in the Posillipo section of Naples. I was more and more settled in the city and playing better and better for the Napoli club. In February '85, we were in the middle of the standings, or the championship, as they called it, but we were undefeated; we were the club that had won more matches than any other team that year. We beat Lazio, four to nothing, I remember, and I scored three of the goals. I had scored eleven so far that season. Just two less than a certain Platini—Michel Platini, that's right—who was driving me nuts. We were just sixteen points away from finishing the season in fifth place and qualifying for the UEFA. It seemed like the perfect time to start putting on the pressure. I had shown them what I had to give; the time had come to play for the Argentine team too. I wanted to play in three earlier exhibition games; I wanted to be with the guys before the first games that mattered. Bilardo kept saying that I was the only sure starter, but he never called.

So I grabbed the reins.

AND MAYHEM BROKE OUT

On Sunday, April 21, after beating Inter Milan, three to one, at San Paolo stadium, I grabbed the mic at the press conference and before anyone asked me any questions, said, "I'll be leaving for Argentina on Sunday, May 5, after the match against Juve, come what may. Not even President Pertini can stop me since he doesn't have the authority to keep the planes from flying out of Rome."

And mayhem broke out.

The next week, on the twenty-eighth, we were playing against Rome at the Olimpico stadium. We tied, one to one, and I vented for a second time after that game: "I want to make myself perfectly clear; I don't want to leave for my country on bad terms, but I desperately need to play with the national team and starting on May 6 I am 100 percent available to Coach Bilardo. You can understand that now, can't you?"

But they couldn't. The Italians didn't get it at all, least of all Matarrese, Antonio Matarrese, who was the president of the Italian Football Federation (Federcalcio). It's true that we had a game scheduled against Udinese—a team at risk of being relegated to a lower division—and the other clubs with a stake in that (teams from Avellino, Como, and Ascoli, I think) complained. But I never said I wasn't coming back! I was willing to play as many games as necessary for Napoli and for the Argentine team. Corrado Ferlaino, the president of the Napoli club, and Rino Marchesi, its coach, weren't thrilled either. But they were getting to know me. And they understood that when I got an idea in my head, nobody could get it out.

On Sunday, May 5, before the game against Juve, I gave another press conference—I was like a president, giving press conferences every day. But the truth is that I was furious because, the Friday before, the federation had sent a telex to the clubs—Napoli in my case and Fiorentina in Passarella's case—saying that we were not allowed to leave the country until the season was over. They threatened us with suspension. Passarella pretended to give in, but not me. That's why I spoke out before the game. "I'm going, whether or not the federation or the club wants me to," I said. I couldn't stay away a second longer. And I said a few other things too: I didn't like them telling us this just a few days before we were scheduled to travel, or the fact that they had let the German players Briegel and Rummenigge travel. I said that they didn't understand anything about the sport: in Argentina, where you sometimes have to play at high altitudes, you have to get there a few days before the match in order to adjust physically. I said that we players had to have a unified response.

If not, these guys in suits would end up running our lives. And that wasn't fair. Not at all.

La Gazzetta dello Sport went to town: "Maradona Challenges the League," the headline read. And on the cover of *Corriere dello Sport*: "Maradona's Uprising. He's Getting on the Plane." You bet I was getting on the plane. No way I wasn't.

For good measure, after the match, which ended in a tie (one to one), I said a few more words: "I said I'll be traveling, and I will be. But I wanted to let you know that on Friday I'll be right back here in order to play against Udinese that Sunday. Then I'll go back to Argentina, but I'll be back for the match against Fiorentina . . . I don't want to hear a word about it from Matarrese or anyone else, for that matter; my club has authorized my trip. I'll spend the next fifteen days going back and forth, but I have no choice. I have never missed a game and I won't miss one now. If you like my decision, I'm glad. If you don't, screw you."

I had made up my mind. To many, it seemed like madness. To me, it was perfect—a challenge to be enjoyed. This, to me, is what it meant to be captain of the Argentine team.

Thinking back on what I did, I can't believe it. But I can say that I would do it all over again without changing a thing.

CARRYING THE TEAM ON MY BACK

The Aerolíneas Argentinas flight, the one I had taken so many times before, left at ten at night. The match against Juve must have ended just after six in the evening, and I had to drive about a hundred and fifty miles to get from Naples to Fiumicino airport in Rome. We had been promised a police escort to get there quicker, but none was sent. I sat down at the wheel of one of my cars, to face the Sunday traffic. I can't remember which car we took: it can't have been the Ferrari because there were too many of us—Jorge Cyterszpiler (my agent); Claudia (my wife at the time); my brother, Lalo, and sister, Lily; and Guillermo Blanco, my press agent—but we went like the wind. I mean, we were flying. I got us there in an hour and a half.

Passarella was waiting at the airport. I got there just after nine, so we had time to talk for a while: "They say that if I don't make it back for those games, they're going to suspend me. What those jerks don't know is that I'm going to make it back to play for them. . . . I'm going to show them once again what Maradona is capable of doing for the Argentine team and also for Napoli."

I fell fast asleep as soon as I sat down in the plane. And the next morning, I was still dreaming, but daydreams. I landed in Buenos Aires and I saw my dad, don Diego, who since the World Cup in Spain had wanted nothing more than to see me wear the Argentine jersey again. We headed for the house in Villa Devoto—the one we still have, where I spent last Christmas, some thirty years later.

I said a few words right there at the airport; I wanted everyone to hear me: "I'm not the savior. I'm Diego. Bilardo is the savior. In fact, his name is Carlos Salvador Bilardo. I'm here to play like any other player, to give the team everything I've got. The game against Juve was brutal, but I am here to play. I promised to come back and I kept my word: here I am."

By four in the afternoon, I was already at the Centro de Empleados de Comercio in Ezeiza where the national team trained back then. I arrived in a tie. For me, playing for the Argentine team again was like going to a party, and I dressed accordingly: faded jeans, pinstriped shirt, tie the same shade of blue as the Argentine flag, blue wool jacket. Pretty as a picture. "Give me two pairs," I said, asking my brother Lalo to hand me the cleats I had picked out to train in. I wanted to break them in. As soon as I arrived, I found out that while I was on the plane the Argentine team had lost another exhibition match, this one against Brazil, in Rio.

These were all signs that I had to go out onto that field and carry the team on my back.

I trained that Monday, Tuesday, and Wednesday alongside the others. And on Thursday, the ninth, we went to Monumental stadium to play against Paraguay. Two years and ten months—almost three years!—later, I put the Argentine jersey back on. I quickly understood that the team needed a lot of work. And it would take time. The goalie was "Pato" Fillol, and the defensive line was Néstor Clausen, Passarella, José Luis Brown, and Oscar Ruggeri. At midfield were Barbitas, "Bocha" Ponce, and Burru. And I was on the offensive line with Oscar Dertycia and Ricardo "El Flaco" Gareca. It was a tie, one to one. I scored the goal at a penalty kick at the end of the first period.

The guys and I really got our focus back, and then at five in the afternoon on the next day I got on a Varig flight for Rome via Rio de Janeiro. On Saturday the eleventh, I was back at Fiumicino, but rather than drive back to Naples, I took another plane and headed to Trieste to play the famous match against Udinese, one of the teams in danger of being relegated to a lower division. We drove the forty miles from Trieste to Udine. I was there in time for dinner, had something to eat, and then went to sleep. And sleep I did! I think I woke up one minute before the game started on Sunday the twelfth. But if any of those knuckleheads in Italy had any lingering doubts, they couldn't say jack after that game: I scored two goals, one of them an amazing free kick. We tied, two to two. What more could they ask of me? I took the quickest shower of all time and got back in the car to drive those forty miles back to Trieste and get on a plane to Fiumicino and then another to Buenos Aires, where I landed on Monday the thirteenth. I don't think I was out of the country long enough for the immigration authorities to stamp my passport.

This time the Argentine team's game was not on a Thursday but on a Tuesday, it was Tuesday the fourteenth, against Chile, once again at Monumental stadium. I didn't have time to train, but it didn't matter. This time it was me and Nery Pumpido on offense, Pato at the goal, and the same defensive line as against the Paraguayans. Russo was added at midfield, and upfield it was Pedrito Pasculli instead of Dertycia. But one thing did not change, mister, and that was me scoring yet another goal, the fourth in six days: one against Paraguay, two against Udinese, and this one against Chile. Burru scored, as well, and we won, two to nothing. I remember the lineups, and you can really see how much things changed later on for the cup. Because people tend to lie about it, and they lie a lot . . .

There was no way Passarella and I could have stayed in Buenos Aires, because the next match in the Italian league was against Fiorentina, where he played. The outcome of the game was not important at all, but the Italians wanted to show us who was boss and demanded we come back. On Saturday the eighteenth I landed back in Rome, and since we were playing at San Paolo stadium that time, I went straight home to get some sleep. I slept almost sixteen hours! I got up and went to the stadium to play—and I mean to play hard. I think my personal rivalry with "El Kaiser" Passarella played a part there, because I gave it my all that day, with two assists in goals that the referee ended up disqualifying and a give-and-go play with Bertoni that ended with Caffarelli scoring a goal. That was my last game with Napoli, and they had nothing to complain about, nothing at all. I left them in eighth place, well out of danger of demotion and only ten points behind Verona, which had been the league champion thanks to the Danish player Preben Elkjaer Larsen and the German Hans-Peter Briegel. I scored fourteen goals, just four less than Platini—but I would catch up to that Frenchman soon enough. They saw me off with bouquets of flowers: that's how grateful they were.

EUROPEANS DON'T HAVE THE SLIGHTEST IDEA

But I had to make another trip, this time to Bogotá, via Frankfurt, to play in a qualifying match with the Argentine team. Between Sunday, May 5, and Monday, May 20, I traveled almost fifty thousand miles. Not bad, huh?

I didn't mind at all. I just wanted to play with the national team. Even back then, the media made up stories about me: they said I had gotten paid eighty thousand dollars for playing in those two games, the one against Paraguay and the one against Chile. Eighty thousand dollars! Come on! You got it all wrong, guys. All I got was the same travel expenses they give everyone: twenty-five dollars per diem. A fortune, right? I told them back then that not even Frank Sinatra brings in that kind of money.

Anyway, I went first class to Bogotá, along with Passarella. He had gotten a warning in one of the league games and so he got out of one of the trips. But this one we took together. We landed in Colombia at night, and I went to have dinner with the guys. I was totally beat, but I wanted to be there.

The next day, we had our first training session at El Campín stadium, and I wanted to be there too. The team for the qualifying rounds was being put together and its first game was against Venezuela, in San Cristóbal stadium. But we were going to spend the whole week in Colombia and head to Venezuela on Friday. That was great news for me—I had been flying so much—but the arrival in San Cristóbal, after landing at the Cúcuta airport, was awful. First off, we took a bus down those mountain roads. And, second, the crowds: I mean, a guy loves his people, but he doesn't want to be killed by them. When we got off the bus heading to the Hotel El Tama, somebody kicked me. I'm sure it wasn't on purpose, but it ended up causing me more trouble than the time Goikoetxea kicked me.

I limped into the hotel and spent the whole night icing my knee. Good thing I didn't have to share a room, because no one would have put up with me. I finally got to sleep at around five in the morning. The pain would be with me straight through the World Cup. And, of course, it was cause for an argument that, thanks to Dr. Oliva, I ended up winning. But that was later—I'll tell you just how it went down, as I never have before, soon enough.

I remember that my dad and brothers, along with Cyterszpiler, came to watch the game. I saw them when I got to the stadium, and they told me that they hadn't been able to find the passes, so they were invited to watch the game from the sidelines. El Turco (my brother Hugo) lost it: "You have no idea the things my brother is going to do today," he said. And I did some of them, I admit, though it wasn't easy. The South American qualifying matches are rough, really rough—as I would find out later, as a coach. Europeans don't have the slightest idea what it's like to play on South American fields against South American teams. None of the fields are easy because your ankles sink straight in. And Venezuela gave us some trouble. It was Sunday, May 26. "Pato" Fillol was the starting goalie, with Clausen and Garré as fullbacks, Passarella as sweeper, and Trossero a little farther upfield; Bilardo put Russo at midfield, to mark players, along with Ponce and Burru; the forwards were Pedrito Pasculli, Gareca, and me.

We got off to a good start: three minutes in, we were winning, one to nothing, with a goal I made from a free kick. But they tied it up at the nine-minute mark because we were careless. Passarella scored in the second period and then right away I headed it in—imagine that, I headed it in! After a free kick by Burru. But then they scored again right away, and we were worried. I didn't like it being so close, not one bit, especially since we would then have to go to Bogotá to take on Colombia, which had beaten Peru in the first of the qualifiers.

It was not yet the Colombia of Carlos "El Pibe" Valderrama, but they did have Willington Ortiz and Arnoldo Iguarán, and they made the most of them. And then there was the problem of the altitude. A lot to deal with. The country's greatness— the Argentine greatness—had to come shining through. By then, being in Bogotá was like playing on the home field, and we could really focus. We had already spent a week there and now we were back. We were settled in at La Fontana hotel— we would be back there later and that would be important before the cup. I had a suite all to myself, no complaints.

My brothers El Turco and Lalo may have been kids, but they knew a ton about soccer. We spent hours and hours together. And since there was a while between games, we had time for barbecues. Of course, my old man was the one at the grill, and my father-in-law, Coco Villafañe, had brought the meat. They may seem small, but things like that mattered; they strengthened the group—a tough group since there were so many would-be leaders.

Some changes were made before the game at El Campín. We had realized some things at the opening match. Ricardo Giusti and Marcelo Trobbiani were placed at midfield: Giusti had done a great job at recovering the ball, and Trobbiani ended up playing upfield near us a lot. It was Sunday, June 2. We won, three to nothing, with two goals by Pedrito and one by Burru. Passarella came up to me at the end of the game and—I'm not sure why—said, in the middle of the field, while we were all celebrating, "Too bad you didn't score, Diego."

"I couldn't care less. All I want is to make it into the cup," I said.

We didn't have experience with qualifying rounds, and we wanted to get it over with. The pressure was enormous. Even today, I think of how we wouldn't have made it to the World Cup if we had lost in Bogotá.

EVERYONE CURSED US OUT

We finally went back to Buenos Aires. From the get-go, we had gotten six out of six points as the visiting team and had scored six goals to boot. I say we "finally" got back, even though, to tell the truth, they didn't treat us very well in Buenos Aires. It was then that I realized how angry people were at the team. It was incredible, actually: they cursed us out until they were hoarse. It was Sunday the ninth. Of course I hadn't been there. I had just played in those two exhibition games and I didn't get what was going on. But I guess people had gone to Monumental stadium to vent their anger. Not at me, but some of the guys (like Trossero, Ricardo "the Gringo" Giusti, and Garré) had a really rough time. It's true that we won, three to nothing, thanks to two goals in the last four minutes of play—one by Clausen, thanks to a pass from me, and one that I headed in—but we smeared the Venezuelans. Russo had scored the first one, and from that moment on, we had them against the goalposts. They had someone marking me, as always—in this case, I think the guy's name was Carrero—and that often worked to my advantage; I have always liked to go one-on-one and to make the guys dance around the field. Besides, it left room for my teammates. This was the first game with Jorge Valdano as a starter, and that gave us the option to kick more high balls. And we were on our way, with great standing, to the only thing we cared about: the World Cup.

One week later, there weren't nearly as many knuckle-heads after our performance at Monumental stadium. We got more applause than boos. Once again, it was Colombia that we measured ourselves up against.

We beat them, one to nothing, with a goal by Valdano—a head shot for a change—but if the goal I almost scored had gone in, I think they would have had to give me two points for it. It was one of the sweetest plays I ever made with the national team. I started out three-quarters upfield and gave the ball a little flick, and all Prince could do was watch me go past. Then, as I was tearing my way upfield, I got around two players, Morales and Quiñónes, I think, to come face to face with Soto. He gave me some trouble, but I managed to get around him and keep making my way upfield. Two others came to get me, Porras on the left and Luna on the right. I faked them both out and went straight between them. I veered over to the left as the goalie made his way over to me, and from there, I gave the ball a powerful kick with my left foot. But Gómez blocked it. On the rebound, Pasculli almost scored. We played good, I mean really good. Then Barbas came in and he fit in perfectly.

By this time, my injured knee—all because of a fan—was a question of state in Italy, mainly in Naples. They even sent Dr. Acámpora, who was the team's doctor, to see how I was doing. After examining me, he said, "We wouldn't have let you play for Napoli in the condition you're in." My answer, to him and to everyone else, couldn't have been clearer: "I've been waiting for the qualifiers and to be captain for two years; I've dreamed of this moment. My knee is not going to keep me from enjoying it. If the Italian doctor tells me not to play, I'll tell him to get on the first plane back to Italy, because I'm playing."

"The Doc," Oliva, was not the only one who came to see me. Pierpaolo Marino, the club's sports director, came as well. Everyone—except for me—was really scared. They examined me one hour before the game, as if I were some kind of exotic bird; the two Italians were there, as was Argentina's team physician Raúl Madero, "El Ciego" Fernando Signorini—who was my trainer and who knew my body better than anyone—and my brother. The knee looked good, but if it hadn't,

I would have played anyway. The story with my knee was just getting started, and I love how it turned out—I'll tell you about that soon enough.

THEN CAME THE GOAL

The business at hand, though, was the qualifying match. Two games against Peru were coming up, one in Lima and one in Buenos Aires, and they were brutal. I can't remember ever suffering on the field the way I did during those two games. For different reasons each time. At the first one, because of how Reyna was marking me, which even today the whole world remembers. He followed me all the way to Havana, the bastard! I mean it, he sent me a ball when I was staying there.

I remember that during the away game, I left the field for a minute so the doc could check me out; Reyna stayed right there at the edge of the field, waiting for me, not even playing. Unbelievable.

It was Sunday, June 23, and we lost, one to nothing, with a goal by Oblitas. I mean, as I said, I liked having a guy on defense marking me closely because I could always get rid of him with a quick move, but that guy was out of hand, like Gentile in '82, who really messed with me. I didn't say a thing: my number-one weapon against that sort of thing has always—and I mean always—been playing.

In soccer today—some thirty years later—Reyna wouldn't have lasted forty-five minutes. And that day he played all ninety. I remember, back at the hotel afterward, telling a journalist how bad I felt—and not only because we had lost. If I had to choose one game to show how hard the qualifiers are, it would be that one. That afternoon Juan Barbas was a starter. We concentrated a bit more on the midfield, and Valdano and I were alone upfield. But it didn't go very well and I started to get worried about what lay ahead. So far, we had done everything well enough. But if something went wrong at the end, it would all go to shit . . .

I swear that a few years back, when we were playing against Peru at Monumental stadium in the qualifiers for South Africa, all those awful images came back to me. I said back then that I had never been so frightened on the field and—wouldn't you know it?—fate put me in the same situation years later. It wasn't that I didn't trust the team or myself, but everything—and I mean everything—seemed to be against us: the field was damp and heavy from the rain, and then out of nowhere the Peruvians started playing like Bayern Munich. It's true that they had really good players, not only Reyna, but also Velásquez, Cueto, Uribe, Oblitas.

That's when you realize how hard it is to be a coach—you want to get out on the field yourself and kick one in there, but you can't. And how hard it is to play hurt. I was exhausted, and my goddamn right knee was killing me. I could play well enough, but I was dreaming about kicking the ball in from an angle and there was no way my knee would let me. I couldn't get the word "playoff" out of my head. "Playoff, playoff . . ." If we lost, we would have to go to the playoffs, and with only ten minutes left, we were behind, two to one.

This was sheer agony!

Camino was in for Clausen that game, and in the first play he kicked Franco Navarro so hard that Navarro was out of the game! Ten minutes in and we were winning, one to nothing, with another goal by Pedrito Pasculli. But then they tied it up and were ahead by the end of the first half. And all the ghosts came back to haunt me.

I felt so powerless I wanted to cry. I kept saying to myself that it was not happening. We were playing so well, easy as pie—and then two goals by them in as many offensive plays. I couldn't make sense of it.

At halftime, we were all cursing one another out. We all knew that we were losing because of our errors, not because of their strengths. Bilardo didn't say a thing in the locker room, not a peep about the goals, how they had happened, what our mistakes had been. He yelled at us to get our shit together and get out there to qualify for the World Cup.

Big mistake on his part.

Because we were nuts by the time we hit the field, and it looked like it would end three to one, not two to two. Time was rushing by. I would look up at the scoreboard and say to myself, "What's going on? Have they sped up the clock?" I remembered the boxer Carlos Monzón looking up at the clock when he was fighting Bennie Briscoe at Luna Park stadium in Buenos Aires. But I wasn't groggy. I couldn't do everything I wanted on the field because of my knee, which was killing me, but we had to qualify.

I was playing farther downfield to try to get the ball and then move upfield and score, but there was a great play—and it wasn't by me. It was three on two: Barbadillo, Uribe, and I don't know who against Trossero and "Pato" Fillol. If Uribe had passed it to Barbadillo, it would have ended three to one—and we would be history. But, faking to one side, Uribe slipped and just nipped the ball. And Pato caught it in the air and we got out of that tight spot.

And now comes the part where we scored.

Passarella finally made a great pass and Gareca just

tapped it in, which was just what happened with Palermo in the qualifiers for South Africa a thousand years later. I always say that when Martín tapped it in with his foot, it was like that play by Gareca. Exactly the same. I went wild in the mud that time, just as I did later when I threw myself down on the grass. The same agony and the same release.

Back when we were still on speaking terms, I remember I once said to Bilardo that he should have taken Gareca to the World Cup in Mexico just as I took Palermo to the World Cup in South Africa. You know why? Because Gareca deserved it because of everything he had done for Bilardo before I was around. I mean, let's admit it, before I hit the scene one of the guys who stood by Bilardo was Gareca. I am talking on an individual level. There were good players, but the one who ended up making the goal was "El Flaco" Gareca. Too bad for me that later, when we played on the team together, he started missing.

But I still remember what I said to Gareca that day in the locker room at Monumental stadium once we had qualified for the cup and were a little—just a little—less anxious: "This is just how it's going to be until the end at the World Cup, man . . . It's going to be agony, but we're going to win it."

We had taken the first step, but I knew that rough times, really rough times, lay ahead. I also knew we were going to be the world champs. Against all odds.

THE DAY MY KNEE BURST

Once I got an idea in my head, it was hard to get it out. Like when my ankle got broken in Barcelona. I picked up the newspaper the next day and read, "He'll never play again." And I went, "Is that so? We'll just see about that."

The same thing happened with my knee after getting kicked in Venezuela—an injury that stayed with me through the qualifiers. They didn't say I was never going to play again—it's true—but they did say I was going to have to have surgery and that the recovery was going to take I don't know how long. But I didn't want to hear any of that, which is why—just like that time in Barcelona—I called Oliva, who was as nuts as he was a great doctor.

And "El Loco" Oliva told me that I wasn't going to need an operation, which was just what I wanted—even needed—to hear.

What had happened? The popliteal muscle was swollen. I learned the word for it at the time and will never forget it—or the pain—until the day I die. I couldn't straighten my leg.

So anyway, after that knucklehead kicked me, every single day I was hearing and reading that Maradona had to have surgery. Everyone had an opinion and the opinion was always the same. Even the doctor for the Naples team had pressured me to have surgery. But not "El Loco" Oliva, not him. It was great to prevail over the doctor from the Inter, from Milan, from Rome, from Juve, all the big-shot doctors who said otherwise. Why the hell did they have to meddle!?

The solution came during an exhibition match we pulled together against a team that Krol coached. Oliva infiltrated my knee and it jammed. "It's going to loosen little by little," he said. But it was time for the game to start and it was still jammed. The game began and, ten minutes in, I had forgotten all about it. I pivoted to run after the ball and—pop!—my knee burst.

I was lying on the ground; it hurt like a motherfucker. So "El Loco" Oliva came over and said, "Did your knee burst?"

"Yeah, doc, it did . . . It's killing me!"

"Great! That's just what I wanted to happen!"

I stared up at him. The guy was even crazier than I thought. I hear him say, "Cover him up," and then he took out a needle—this huge needle—and he infiltrated my knee in the middle of the field. I was in tremendous pain.

"Now move your knee," he told me.

And I moved it, no trouble at all. It had unjammed. I kept playing. I think I even scored. We won, two to nothing. I played the whole ninety minutes and when I got to the bench, El Loco says to me, "And what about all those guys who said we had to operate? Where are they now?"

WE WERE GOING TO GIVE IT OUR ALL

Okay, so my problem was taken care of. Now we had to take care of the rest, all the team's other troubles.

The team had to connect with the fans. They weren't into us, not one bit. As I said, it was an unpopular team because of the coach we had and the team he had played for. They were talking a lot of dirt about us and a lot of knuckleheads jumped on that bandwagon.

But we players were the ones who were having a rough time of it; we were taking it from all sides. So I put myself out there. Besides, now that my knee had healed, I was having some magical times on the field, playing for Napoli. In late '85—I think it was November—I made a dream come true for the whole city: we beat Juve thanks to a goal I scored from a free kick—Tacconi, the keeper, is still looking for the ball. It was an indirect free kick from within the penalty area, above the wall of defensive players. And this was way before the refs started spraying foam to keep the defense players on the wall from moving until the ball was kicked. The only thing on the grass during that match was sawdust! There was a lot of talk of all this not long ago, because of the thirtieth anniversary and because, just like old times, Napoli was causing trouble for Juve. As far as I'm concerned, they can break all standing records and outplay me. If Naples is happy, I'm happy.

I was doing great at Napoli back then, but the Argentine team was struggling. Just to be perfectly clear about how I feel for the national team, I'm going to say again now what I said thirty years ago: if I had been forced to choose between Napoli and the Argentine team, I would have stuck with the Argentine team. It was time to step up.

Maybe that's why, as the headline of *El Gráfico* sports magazine said, I felt alone, sad, and worried. I remember that cover all right. It was not long before the World Cup, and Bilardo had come to Naples to see me. He spent the whole time asking me how I was doing physically. I don't know what he was thinking—that I wasn't going to keep my word, that I wasn't going to train? It bugged me. And it bugged me even more when he went to Florence to talk to Passarella about the whole thing, as if the issue weren't settled. You know what he was afraid of? He was afraid that everything we had agreed on would change suddenly when we had almost reached our goal, which was simply to play in the World Cup. I mean, at times I felt like throwing in the towel. I had had it. I had grown a beard, and everyone said that that was a bad sign. It's true that I was not looking my best, but my sister, Lily, had told me to try growing a beard. She said it would make me look more masculine. I was a tough guy as long as I had my mother by my side. Because at that time my mother, Tota, had come to Italy to spend a few days with me and I would say to her, "What about you and me heading back to Buenos Aires together, Tota? What do you say?"

Again, it's not that I was scared, but I was aware that I had a lot on my plate and not everything was going the way I wanted. A bunch of annoying exhibition games were coming up, first against France and then against Napoli—my Napoli—and against the Swiss team Grasshopper. In the locker room after training one day, Eraldo Pecci, a teammate of mine, messed with me, saying I was afraid of making a fool of myself against the French. I didn't think it was funny, not one bit. I wanted to punch him out!

I also wanted Bilardo to stop messing around and to decide who was on the World Cup team. There were some thirty possible players and he had to choose twenty-two. I'm not saying he had to define the entire roster but cut it down, as a vote of confidence to the ones who would be playing on the team. And to the ones who had put up with all sorts of crap. I had gone through thick and thin with the guys who had played in the qualifiers, and I would have done anything for them, guys like Gareca, Pasculli, Camino, Garré, Burru, "Bocha" Ponce, and even "Pato" Fillol and Valdano, no matter how experienced they were. What I really wanted was for Bilardo to show us some respect as men more than as players. And for him to add more men later, if necessary, but for them to be men. Guys like "Tolo" Gallego, whom I loved, and "Guaso" Domenech, who pulled himself up from under. It was not a cast of phenomenal players, of miracle workers, out there on the field. But these were guys who gave it their all out there, who worked as hard as anyone could. That's why I said publicly I would like Bilardo to give Ramón Díaz a chance. That's right, Ramón Díaz. I said so before the '86 cup and also in '90. So all that stuff about me deciding who would be on the team—just a crock. I mean, Barbas, who was like a brother to me, was not going to be on the World Cup roster!

The guy who was always on the edge, with one foot in and one foot out, was "El Bocha," Ricardo Bochini. As everybody knows, it was my dream as a kid to play with him, but that never—or almost never—happened. He rocked it on a tour I was not a part of and then he lost it and quit the team. It was not until the end of '85 that we met up in some exhibition games against Mexico in Los Angeles. I think he helped the team, no matter how nuts he was at the time. The same with Claudio "Bichi" Borghi. He was just a kid and sometimes he would say—or kick, like in that first exhibition game against France—too much. We didn't make fools of ourselves the way Pecci said we would, but they beat us, two to nothing. Borghi got thrown out of the game for kicking Luis Fernández, I think. Passarella ended up playing, but it was a miracle that he didn't get thrown out too, because he elbowed Tigana in the worst way. Three days later we played against Napoli in San Paolo stadium. What can I say? For me, it was really strange to play against my teammates at that stadium, but it was only an exhibition game. That was the first time Bilardo put Passarella in as a sweeper and Ruggeri and Garré in as stoppers—something he wouldn't do again for a long, long time.

Then we went to Switzerland to play against Grasshopper

Club in Zurich. We just barely beat them, one to nothing. I don't know what those games were for, really. I mean, if we won, it didn't mean shit, and if we lost, they would say we sucked. I didn't understand that about Bilardo. And they didn't understand us either—didn't understand me—when I told them to give us a little more time. Just a little more time, for God's sake! We'd show them what we were really made of when we were all together in Mexico.

They were worried about the physical training, for example, but I knew perfectly well how I was training and how I was going to train. They said that the Europeans ran more than us, that they were stronger. But I was sure that in Mexico it was going to be different, really different. I knew we were going to be able to do what we wanted. We forwards, for example, would really stick to marking and not stay put when we lost possession of the ball.

Criticism has always made me stronger. If they said that Maradona was just another player, it egged me on; it didn't beat me down. But that's not how it is for everybody. If you believed what they told you, Borghi was no longer so promising, and Pasculli couldn't score a goal against anyone . . . That's why I said we were a persecuted team.

In April, Bilardo finally handed in the final list. And he didn't pay much attention to my suggestions. Gareca didn't make it, neither did "Pato" or Barbas. At least he called Héctor Enrique, who was a great player. He had only let him play once before, in Toulon, but he had never played with us in the big league, and it came as a surprise. A bunch of the guys wanted to kill Bilardo when he released the list, including Barbas, Trossero . . .

In the end, it was Pumpido, Islas, and Zelada as goalies;

Brown, Clausen, Cucciuffo, Garré, Olarticoechea, Passarella, and Ruggeri on defense; Batista, Borghi, Bochini, Burruchaga, Enrique, Giusti, Tapia, and Trobbiani as midfielders; Almirón, Pasculli, and Valdano as forwards. And me as captain!

We did another tour and it did not go well, not at all. They really laid into us when we lost to Norway! Then we scored seven goals against Israel, but that wasn't enough—it was never enough.

But it was enough for me. I was sure that if they left us players in peace, if they let us train—as a team and individually—the way we wanted to in Mexico, we would be up to the task of winning the World Cup.

I loved that team. I loved it deeply and in a special way. I felt a part of it. I was the captain of an amazing group of guys. I once said that what we needed was luck, but I was wrong. What we needed was hard work . . . And respect. Respect of us, for the players. And a lack of respect—that was one thing I was not willing to put up with.

But the one thing I asked was that they give us, the players—me and everyone else—time. I didn't want to be the captain of the worst national team of all time, as I said back then. A lot of people let what the journalists were saying get to them. But if they left us, the players, in peace, we would be able to make it happen. I had gotten much stronger in Italy: they had to kick me hard if they wanted to bring me down. I was preparing myself, training hard. But they were aiming the firing squad at us on every side.

It was then, after that goddamn tour, that the government announced they wanted to get rid of Bilardo. It was awful. And I came out to back him up—and I still do today.

Some thirty years ago, I did for Bilardo what, after the 2010 World Cup, he failed to do for me.

But at least it was good for something. Because, at that point, there was no more time for words. It was time to get out there and play. And we players were going to give it our all.

CHAPTER 2

At Those Meetings, the Champions Were Born

In Colombia, a major revolution started brewing, one that put an end to Bilardo's iron rule and began to show how tough the team was. Because, until then, if Bilardo said, "We have to go to Timbuktu," we—or the rest of the guys, really—would all get up and go to Timbuktu, no questions asked. He would say, "We have to play that game, not this one," and we would play that game and not this one, like during that weird tour he put together with games in Bogotá and in Barranquilla, even though we had already been at the training camp at Club América in Mexico for over ten days by then (early May '86).

And—no way, man—that's not how it should go down.

In the end, we only played one match in that tour. Just one on the field. We fought some battles off the field, though. And those turned out to be much more important.

And that was thanks, in large part, to us, the players, and to a meeting we had in this enormous suite in La Fontana hotel in Bogotá the very night we flew in from Mexico; we had another meeting in Barranquilla after a zero to zero tie against Junior.

The first meeting was on a Tuesday, the thirteenth, which they say is bad luck in Argentina, but it was not at all unlucky for us. We got together as soon as we landed in Colombia, and it was on that night in May, when the opening of the World Cup was still three weeks away, that a champion team began coming together, one that was not going to be pressured by anybody. A team that would make itself heard by anyone and everyone: reporters, chronically bitter fans, politicians, officials, naysayers (who were everywhere), and even the coaching staff. In a word, a team with balls.

NO COSMIC KITE HERE

We had been in Mexico for a week and were leaving for Colombia that morning. Everything went wrong. We were supposed to take off at eight thirty—which was already a pain in the ass—but the flight didn't get off the ground until noon because of a bomb threat or something. So we were pissed by the time we did take off, which just heated things up even more at the meeting that night.

It was just us, the twenty-two players. That's it. Nobody else.

We talked about money, about the bonus we would get if we won the cup . . . That's right, because we believed we were going to win it all, and we knew we wouldn't make jack even if we ran the victory lap. Do you know how much we got for being world champions thirty years ago, which was the last time the Argentine team won the World Cup? Thirty-three thousand dollars. That's right! That's just travel expenses for a player today. And do you know what we got for travel expenses? That's right! Twenty-five dollars! Just twenty-five bucks! I still can't believe it.

We talked about that at the meeting, but the truth is that we didn't give a shit about the cash. We were there for much more than that. It was rough, because some of us were already earning good money for playing in Europe, but not all of us. Some of the guys didn't even have decent cleats; no one sponsored them the way they do now. What I wanted was for them to understand that the Argentine jersey was worth far more than that, and that the Argentine jersey would be on *our* backs—it would be us, not the usual suit-wearing backstabbers or naysayers, who would be wearing the jersey. Just us.

We talked about the training sessions, about what we needed, about giving it our all and then some, giving everything!

I remember it like it was yesterday. I stood up in the middle of the room and started talking. I looked all the guys in the eye and felt like my blood was boiling and the vein on the back of my neck was about to explode. I ground my teeth so hard I thought they were going to crack. My fist was clenched as I spoke, like I was going to punch someone. That's what I felt like doing. But the blows—aimed straight at the heart—were words.

"What we have to do now is forget about everything. And I mean everything. Our clubs, our families, money, our troubles. The only thing we have to think about is us. Nobody else. Just us! And it doesn't matter who's a starter and who's a sub—don't bother me with that crap. We have to work together like hand and glove, be willing to sell our souls to help a teammate. And that goes for every one of us, and I mean every last one! If one of us wins, we all win—got it? Because a lot of folks are expecting us—and I mean every last one of us—to lose. And they think that when we lose, we will be torn apart more than they have already torn us apart. And, you know what? We are not going to give them that pleasure. No way!"

That was my oath.

And if we had gone out on the field right then, we would have scored five goals no matter who we were up against. It was us against everyone else, against the whole world. Some of the guys were just kids. But everyone spoke up. Each of us, in his own way, spoke his mind. What that group needed was to come together, to talk, to be able to talk. Even Bochini talked that day—we had barely heard his voice. So did Enrique, who had joined the team just a month before. Zelada talked, and he didn't become part of the team until we got to Mexico; Almirón, who wouldn't see even a minute of play, spoke, and of course Valdano said his bit—sometimes we had to tell him to keep quiet. "Enough!" we would shout at him. Passarella spoke up too that time, but not after that—you'll know why soon enough.

And so, after the game against Junior in Barranquilla, when we were too exhausted to run another step, we started asking ourselves what we were doing there instead of in Mexico. There were only three weeks to go before the World Cup; it didn't make any sense for us to be running around Colombia, where we would, most likely, have to deal with criticism and even run the risk of being injured by players on the other team who wanted to show how tough they were. The weather conditions were different—it was hot and humid, which meant a whole different set of problems from the altitude we would have to deal with later on. I remember that Goyén, the Uruguayan player, did a really good job as goalie that game, which ended one to one—but we should have won it. But what I remember most is how exhausted we were, that we would just watch the players on the other team run by; I remember Uribe running circles around us. We didn't play that bad, not as bad as we had been playing. In fact, I think we played pretty good. But we were beat. We couldn't get it in the net. And for a team that so few believed in, that was awful.

We talked to "El Profe" Echevarría, the team's trainer—a master, the best guy on the coaching staff. And, very wisely, he understood when we told him we had decided to go back to Mexico. I went to talk to Bilardo myself after putting it to the whole team and making sure they agreed. I went to Bilardo, and he started in saying that the game was all planned and this, that, and the other. But the second game hadn't been played yet. Who knows what was agreed but I believe that he might have been getting a cut or something, because the exhibition games were organized by Enzo Gennoni, who was a friend of his. Anyway, we had played the first game in Barranquilla, which was at sea level and thus useless to us in terms of getting ready for Mexico. They said the second game would be played in Bogotá, which was higher up at least, but there was no way we were going.

I confronted him. "Listen, Carlos, the team is not going. We can barely stand up from the heat, and we run the risk of being injured by the other team and demoralized by the naysayers. What good is it, at this point, to play a game at sea level? It's totally pointless, not good for shit. And it's not like we're going to play at the same altitude in Bogotá either. We'll go to Bogotá all right, but just to catch the plane back to Mexico."

"Come on! There's an extra ten thousand in it for you," he tried to convince me.

But it wasn't about ten thousand for me or for anybody when all we got for an exhibition game was eight hundred dollars—that's right, just eight hundred bucks! What we had to do was get back to the training camp, rest up, and get used to the climate despite all the criticism that was coming our way, which only made matters that much worse. We needed to train in the city where we were going to play and where you would feel like your lungs were splitting in two after running just a few steps. The altitude in Bogotá wasn't as low as in Barranquilla, of course, but it wasn't as high as Mexico City either.

It did the group good to win that battle against Bilardo. It wasn't easy, but he had to give in. We threatened not to play, and we wouldn't have, either.

That was the breaking point. I had called the whole group together and now it was stronger. That's when we decided that it was us against the world, so we had to stick together. And stick together we did!

We were the first team to arrive and we wanted to be the last to leave. I have never liked training camps—I always feel like they cramp my style—but this time it was different, because we had come clean with one another and looked each other in the eye and said what we felt. From then on, everything came together.

After that trip, I spoke with Cóppola, Guillermo Cóppola. "Do you remember in Israel when I told you we might be able to finish third?"

"Yes, of course."

"Well, in Barranquilla I had an even stronger feeling. I felt like we were real good, too good. I had the feeling we could be world champions."

What I didn't tell him was that I felt that way, not because of what had happened on the field, during the game, but because of everything that had happened off the field. Because of everything we had worked out by saying things straight, the way it should be.

There was a divide between the Bilardo camp, on the one hand, and the Menotti camp, on the other. And now I can say with perfect calm that I am and have always been with Menotti. But I was the captain and had to carry the flag for the group. Cosmic kite or no cosmic kite, my goal was for us to be the world champions, no matter who our coach was.

That's why I said at a certain point that Passarella didn't play because he was in the Menotti camp. He wanted to heighten the differences between us, and what we had to do—the one thing we had to do—was stick together. The differences were crystal clear. Menotti could capture a game in two words, whereas Bilardo had to show ten videos to explain a single play. But we were all together for one purpose. We had to stop fucking around.

The declared Menotti supporters were Passarella, "El Bocha" Bochini, and Valdano—there weren't many of them because, except for a few guys he could not overlook, Bilardo made sure to choose players who did not support Menotti. Ruggeri was one of them. I mean, he couldn't leave Ruggeri out. He was a soccer giant!

I was another guy he couldn't leave out. He had chosen me, and the only thing I cared about was the final goal. It still hurt that I had not been on the '78 team and that we didn't make it in '82. The only thing I cared about was the Argentine team becoming the world champions. Everything else was, for me, secondary, a waste of time. But all this—and some other things as well—was already in the air before the meetings started.

It was us, the players, who won the meeting in Bogotá, and the meeting in Barranquilla too. From then on, there was no Menotti camp or Bilardo camp. We were tired and all we wanted to do was get back to Mexico. We were up until like four in the morning changing our tickets, and "El Profe" Echevarría was right there with us; he understood us better than anyone.

YOU GOT THAT, YOU BACKSTABBER?

Those weren't the only meetings, as I said. We had a bunch of them. To talk about how the team was doing, to make sure we were feeling all right, to see if we had any unmet needs or if we wanted to train more, to assess if El Profe had to work with a player on his game or on overall conditioning . . . We would have those meetings every so often; the group—we players—organized them, and they were important to making us stronger. No one else was allowed in, not the coaching staff, not anyone.

But the "Passarella meeting"—that was what we all called it—happened after those meetings in Colombia; it took place in Mexico, at the training camp, as soon as we got back from the tour. It was at that meeting that things really came together.

I told the story in my book, *Yo soy el Diego de la gente* (*I Am Diego of the People*), but I am going to tell it again—and in more detail—to set the record straight. Because every part of my body may have been injured, but not my memory. My memory is in perfect shape.

This is how it went. "The rebels"—that's what Passarella called Pasculli, Batista, Islas, and me—were fifteen minutes late to I don't know what. We had gone out because we had some free time. I mean, we were just fifteen minutes late! But that was reason enough to have to get lectured to by the dictator Passarella. It was just like him: "How can the captain, of all people, be late?" and so on and so forth.

I let him finish even though my vein was popping out of my neck I was so angry, but I held it in. "Are you done?" I asked. "Yes," he said, all snotty. "Okay, now let's talk about you a little," I said.

And right there, in front of the whole team, I described just what he was like, everything he had done. I didn't hold back. I said every last thing I knew about him. I would rather be a junkie, hard though that is, than be an opportunist or a bad friend. And I say "bad friend" because of what he did that ended up pushing me away from him and making him what he was in the eyes of everyone: when he was in Europe, everyone knew that he would take these little getaways to Monaco. We suspected it was to see the wife of a teammate, another player on the Argentine team. According to Pecci he would brag about it in the locker room of the Fiorentina club. The truth is that by this stage no one could stand him.

And it was a big—and I mean a big—mess because on the team there were two groups. The ones who backed Passarella, his group—guys like Valdano, Bochini, and others. Passarella had got it in their heads that we were late because we were doing coke and this, that, and the other—but mostly that part about doing coke. And then there was my group.

So I said, "Okay, Passarella, I admit that I use." A tremend-ous silence set in. I went on, "But there's something else going on here. I wasn't late because I was doing coke. I wasn't. And be-sides, you are implicating other people, the guys who were with me, and they don't have anything to do with it. You got that, you backstabber?"

What was really going on was that Passarella wanted to win the team over like that, by causing trouble and making up stories, by throwing a wrench into things. He had wanted to win them over ever since they hadn't named him captain and he'd lost his position of leadership; he had been waiting for his chance. It's true, he was a good captain, and I have al-ways said so. But I outdid him because I was, am, and will al-ways be the one and only true captain.

After that, he tried to get me any way he could. He would go up to Valdano and talk to him for like four hours, not let-ting the poor guy get a word in edgewise. Valdano is a very smart guy and someone that everyone—myself included—listened to. Anyway, Passarella got it in Valdano's head that because of me, all the players were using drugs. That's right, that's what he said! So I stood there, right in the middle of the meeting, and in the name of my teammates and of myself—of course—I started screaming at him. "Nobody here is using, man. You got that?"

And I swear on my daughters that while we were in Mex-ico, none of us was using.

When Valdano came to ask me for an explanation and to give me a lecture about what I could and could not do, thinking—because of everything Daniel had said to him—that I was doing drugs, I stopped him in his tracks and said,

"Hold on a minute, Jorge, for Christ's sake. Whose side are you on? Are you saying that anything Passarella tells you is true and anything I tell you isn't?"

A bit calmer, he said, "Okay, tell me your side."

"No, wait, we're going to have another meeting."

So we went to the dining hall, because at the training camp there was nowhere else to get together and talk. And it was there that, right in front of Passarella, I said everything I knew about him. Once again, a thick silence. And he didn't say a goddamn thing. I mean, what could he say, it was as if he was made of stone. What he didn't know was that I had gotten my hands on a list of long-distance calls that the team had to pay for, and he was the one who had made all the calls.

"By the way, what about that two-thousand-peso phone bill we all have to pay for because no one has owned up to making the calls. Who made them?"

Nobody said a word. Some guys looked down at the ground. It was dead silent. What Passarella didn't know was that at that time—in 1986, some thirty years ago—telephone bills in Mexico were itemized. And it was his number, the bastard! He was earning like two million dollars a year and he played dumb about a phone bill for two thousand.

The situation exploded. I mean, I could have covered the bill myself, but so could Passarella, and he was making us all pitch in to pay for his calls. And he thought it would never come to light, that he would get away with it. "Look, Passarella, all these calls are yours. There's not one call of mine to Naples, not one call of Valdano's to Madrid, no call anywhere else—just your calls . . . every last one of them."

And from then on they all stood behind me. I mean, the guy was a monster, the kind of guy who was bringing in millions but wanted to make the rest of us pay. A stubborn piece of shit is what he was. And that was when the divide between the Maradona camp and the Passarella camp came down to twenty-one against one. "Bocha" Bochini talked to him, but just because he was sort of nuts. The rest of the players backed me. Imagine Brown, who didn't even play for a team! Islas, Pumpido, even Zelada—they all lined up to take a shot at Passarella.

Even Valdano got pissed. "You're a piece of shit!" he screamed at El Kaiser.

And Passarella fell apart. He got diarrhea—Montezuma's revenge—but actually we were all pissing out of our assholes. Then he pulled a muscle and couldn't play in the cup. But the team realized that he didn't want to play.

Like a bunch of fools, we went to visit him to keep him company. We even played cards with him because he was feeling bad—we all were, actually. I asked Pasculli, "How's your shit holding up, Pedrito?" And he told me that he was pissing out of his asshole, like all of us. Passarella made a big deal out of it, getting an IV and all. They took him back to Buenos Aires until two days before our first game, which was against South Korea. And then he pulled his calf muscle!

Come on!

We wanted to go after him in the locker room, to beat him to a pulp. He was a traitor: not only did he want to make the guys pay for his calls, but he didn't want to play with his teammates who had even gone to visit him at the hospital. And now during a warm-up that my grandson could do, he pulls his calf?

Bullshit!

Then he even went to Acapulco to catch some rays. And some wise guy put a photo of him and his wife up on the board where Bilardo was going to give instructions—you know, with a bunch of useless arrows all over the place—for the game against England. If, today, Daniel had the chance to go up to the guys and ask them one by one, they would all say that he had made a mistake by not playing. And they would also say that that was the moment when the divide between the Menotti and the Bilardo camps broke; that is, the moment when everyone came together. Because those of us who backed Menotti also backed Bilardo. I mean, what was Bilardo going to say to me? "Play the left," "Play the right," "Play left fullback," or "Play wherever you want"? "El Flaco" Menotti would have said the same.

And I say that now. I tell it just like it happened and just like I saw it, knowing that at that time Menotti was not going out on a limb for me in his statements.

And all these years later, I still see it the same. Passarella never accepted that I was the only sure starter and that I was the captain of Bilardo's team. And so he started turning up the pressure. In an article published in *El Gráfico* sports magazine in October '85, he said, "If I'm not a sure starter, I'm not playing."

By then, I was sick of all the gossip and jealousy, of all the petty bullshit. I went on the warpath. I held a press conference in Naples in which I didn't hold back. I spoke as captain, though not like the sole owner of the truth, and I didn't consult Bilardo or Passarella beforehand. I was caught in the middle there. For Bilardo, it seemed, the only sure starter was Maradona. I thought Bilardo had been clear about that from the get-go, but I didn't know what Daniel thought. The only thing I could say to him as a friend—and I thought I was his friend off the field—as a teammate and as a player, was that it was essential that he respect each player's track record. Daniel knew that Bilardo had respected us from the time he called us for the qualifiers. I don't know what promises Bilardo may or may not have made. That was between them, and they had to work it out.

But because of everything I read about it and what my mom told me on the phone from Buenos Aires, I am still convinced that something fishy was going on.

Passarella wanted to be a sure starter. Everyone—I mean, those who had been by his side and seen him fight like a lion for the Argentine jersey—knew that he was a born winner. So what I didn't understand was why he put us through so much, threatening to quit the team when nobody wanted him to, not even Bilardo?

Every coach has his favorites. Under Menotti, if anyone touched Passarella, they had to call in the national guard. And we all understood that, because he was the captain, everyone's darling, just as Houseman had been before that, and nobody said anything. I once quit the national team when Menotti was coach because, at that time, I thought we should all be at the same level. But then I went back. That's why I didn't want to say anything to Passarella about him leaving; he was an adult and I wasn't going to go around telling him what to do. The only thing I could ask of him as his captain and as his teammate was that he work things out with Bilardo as best he could. At the training camp, he knew that he was going to be a starter, because he was a leader, with all that meant on the field and off. We needed him—the whole country needed him. And that was all I cared about. But I was the captain.

What I asked Passarella was that he do what was best for him, not for us. I knew him well, and that's why I think there was something strange behind the whole thing, even though I wasn't sure what. If I had known, I would have said something, because I've always liked things to be out in the open.

I didn't know—and I didn't want to know—if this was just a whim of Bilardo's or what, but we always respected what the coach said. I asked myself why things should be any different. Because he was one of the twenty-two players, and deep down he knew what he gave to the team. Passarella didn't need Bilardo to say "You're a starter." I mean, he had always been a starter. All I know is what Bilardo said to him at that time: "The question of who's captain is not an issue. I started from scratch as a coach, without taking into account what happened before . . . And I believe that, starting at the qualifiers, Maradona should be the captain. He is the man who best represents Argentina in the world. I don't understand why Passarella is so upset."

And Passarella, catty like he is, didn't help much when he said, "What Bilardo told me—even though I already knew it— is that he believes Maradona should be the captain. I told him that I respected his decision because he is the coach; he has the last word on this."

All I knew is that we had to be more united than ever. We couldn't afford to bicker! Passarella was putting on the pressure and I wasn't going to allow it. We couldn't go on with the divide between the Menotti supporters and the Bilardo supporters. We were really going after one another, and it wasn't right. And I knew what I was talking about. I mean, I had been flagrantly left out of the '78 World Cup—I still believe I should have been on that team. I'm not going to name names, but there are three guys I could have replaced on the team. And in '82 I resigned as captain of the U-20 national team, a post Menotti had given me in '79. I mean, "El Flaco" Menotti had the authority to make the decision, and I am eternally grateful for what he did for me.

And in the middle of that big mess, I had had a run-in with Passarella on the field: Napoli against Fiorentina, in Florence, on October 13, 1985. All week the Italian newspapers were going on and on about the great duel, the fight. "Daniel, ricorda che adesso sono tuo capitano" ("Daniel, Remember That I'm Your Captain Now") read the headline. Powerful shit.

They asked me if I had discussed the captain issue with Passarella. "No, we're adults. There is no need to talk about it when it makes perfect sense. Daniel is a smart guy. Besides, where is it written that you are captain for life?" I said. I admit that was kind of a sneaky thing to say, but Passarella avoided the whole thing, saying, "Since I am, for the time being, not on the Argentine team, I'd rather not discuss it."

The game ended in a tie, zero to zero. We shook hands afterward, and I said what I really believed at the time: he was, in my view, an unquestionable starter on the Argentine team. I mean, that should have been enough, right? What else did he want? But the story was far from over.

The truth is, I've always respected Passarella a great deal as a player. But when they made me captain, he didn't even take the trouble to congratulate me. That was the first thing that seemed off. "He must be pissed," I thought. And that's when the distance between us started.

It was good to let it out, because later Valdano and I talked about it a lot, and we even got close. And the whole Passarella thing had come to a close—mostly, there were still a few details to lay to rest, but later, once we were in Mexico at the training camp.

MEXICAN HATS

By the time *El Gráfico* put that famous photo with us in the sombreros on the cover, I really felt like the captain, and I thought Passarella was history. That meant that, as captain, I wanted to do the shoot: "You didn't congratulate me? Okay, now I'm going to rub your face in my captain's armband. It's right there, on my left arm." This, for me, was living it up, because the captain was the one who got to negotiate player bonuses, the guy at the head of the group, the one who told "El Profe" Echevarría what to look into. Who the leader really was had been clear from day one, but now there was no denying it. I admit that I had followed Passarella closely. Of course I had! I mean, he was thirty-three and I was just twenty-five at the time. Of course I respected everything he had done. But if I respect you, I expect you to respect me too, man. Show me some respect! And the truth is he had a hard time doing that.

So things went down at the photo shoot. I asked what he had said when they invited me to be in the shoot. And I know that he asked what I had said. So there we were, both right on time for it, at the training field.

As soon as they brought in the bags with the hats, I grabbed one with a dark-yellow band on it, like the stripe on the Boca club jersey. I left him a deep-red one: "That one has the River color. Put it on," I said. I tried to ease the tension a bit, but you could tell he was nervous. He was not at all pleased that we were getting the same treatment. I mean, let's make it perfectly clear: the journalists were asking him why he was not assured a starter position and I was. Take a look at the archive and you'll see it. I mean, he was a hard hitter by then, and they were still a bit wary of me.

We did the picture and, as always, the guy who kept us laughing was "El Profe" Echevarría, who couldn't believe his eyes. His laughter was infectious and pretty soon we were all cracking up. Passarella said that he didn't want to open his mouth much because his bottom teeth were all crooked—which was about as genuine as a blue dollar bill. I felt on top of the situation, which is why, I think, he didn't want to hang around and talk after the photo shoot. He said that the training session started at six and he wanted to be on time. But it wasn't six yet. We had time to hang out. I hung around.

WHERE DID THEY GET THE IDEA THAT I THOUGHT I WAS GOD?

In an interview I said that I would love to be the best player in the '86 World Cup and that I was at the top of my game, ready to make that happen. But, right away, I clarified, "Provided that Argentina also has a great cup." I mean, the two went hand in hand: great players are backed by great teams.

And a journalist said that I thought I was the God of soccer. Sometimes I had to put up with such bullshit! Where did he get that idea? There were no kings or gods. All the team wanted was to do justice to the history of Argentine soccer. The Europeans were saying we would finish in the top five, and in Argentina some people were saying we would be home after the first round. And that hurt, because we needed their support.

It would have helped us to have that support, but since we didn't, the group found other ways to grow stronger. Like those meetings. We would get together whenever we had the chance, to talk things through. And though it was rough, that first meeting in Colombia had been positive.

It was different back then, and some things seem so stupid from today's perspective. Those of us who were playing for European clubs, for example, knew that we had to get an injection each morning to strengthen our livers.

But the guys who played in Argentina weren't used to that. Sometimes one of the guys would get annoyed and ask what good it really did, and we had to explain it to him. There was debate about things that should have been completely routine, but that's what the group was like. I'm not saying that we would argue over an injection, but the idea was to get tighter and tighter as a team.

And for me that was what mattered most: to be of one mind. There might have been guys who thought I didn't know what I was doing, but that's not how it was, not at all. I thought everything over. I wanted a really tight team because I knew what we would be up against would be rough, real rough. We were forging a group, the group.

That's why I gave an ear to everyone who came to see me, even when they came to tell me what they wanted in a captain. Valdano, for example. What Jorge didn't know was that I had been preparing for this since the time I was a kid playing for the Cebollitas.

Many thought I wasn't the right choice for captain because I was always taking so much shit; they would just come after me and sock it to me. But I didn't react to any of that stuff! And anyone who still had the image of the guy I was in Spain in '82, when I kicked that Brazilian player Batista in the balls, was clueless. Four years had gone by! Did they think I hadn't learned anything? I was the captain of Napoli. And of the Argentine national team. I wasn't the sort of guy who lost his head all the time over nothing. I could take it and keep going; I had learned how to talk to the referee.

And, you know what? The captain's armband wasn't a burden or a responsibility for me. Just the opposite! It was no burden: it gave me strength. I had talked about this in Italy with Enrique "El Cabezón" Sívori, and I had seen it in Passarella. But I believed in myself and in my approach to being captain. Talking everything through, for instance. Being captain meant not putting the blame on anyone, not going behind anyone's back. If there is something to say, say it straight to their face. That was my style. And it was the style I wanted for the team. That is why I called that meeting. Say it to my face, man.

The opening of the cup was less than a month away. The only thing left to do was train hard to start out at the top of our game. We knew just what we wanted. But we also knew where we were coming from. And nothing had come easy, nothing at all.

CHAPTER 3

Stick It to Maradona

ARGENTINA 3, SOUTH KOREA 1
—Mexico City, Monday, June 2

When we landed in Mexico on May 5, the headlines read "The World Cup Has Begun." We got a hero's welcome! The cameras from Televisa would follow us everywhere. Naturally, we were the first ones to arrive—there was still a month before the first match. But for me the cup had begun long before.

Starting in March, no matter where I was playing for Napoli, I would travel to the Italian Olympic Committee's medical center in Rome. Fernando Signorini, an amazing trainer and great guy, had read up on how Italian cyclist Francesco Moser had broken a record at high altitude in Mexico in '84. Earlier, in January, he had taken me to see some guys in Milan. He asked them so many questions that I finally said, "Ciego, quit it with all the questions or they're going to think you don't know what you're talking about." But they were the ones who told me that the key guy was Professor Dal Monte, Antonio Dal Monte. A phenomenon. He was the chief scientist in Italian sports, and he knew Enzo Bearzot, the coach of the Italian national team, very well.

In fact, Dal Monte told us that Bearzot had been with him in Mexico when Moser broke the record. But he wasn't interested in working on his team.

"Screw them. They'll be back after the first round," I said.

"For me, it would be incredible to have a chance to train you," he said.

With that, he won me over.

"When do we start?" I asked.

"Next Monday . . ."

"The cup's three months away. Is there enough time?"

"You'll arrive in the best shape of your life."

I liked the plan. It started out with a general assessment, followed by training sessions, and ended with "the best shape" Dal Monte had promised for the cup. So I said, "What the hell, let's go for it, brother." And the truth is, I was in amazing shape when the cup started. They did things at that center they didn't do anywhere else. I was strong, real strong. I mean, if you look at the photos from back then, I look like a boxer, with strong arms, pecs—a nice-looking kid. And I was fast. I would fly through the air. It would be either my World Cup or Platini's. I felt that physically I would be able to shine in Mexico—more than elsewhere, even—if I was in good shape. If we were at sea level, they might be able to catch me, but if I was in shape, that wouldn't be so easy in Mexico. The altitude ended up working in my favor.

By then, my old agent Cyterszpiler was gone, and Guillermo Cóppola was helping me take care of business. But I'm not going to talk about all that now. I've already said what I have to say. What's the point of talking about it again now? The ones who needed to know what they did and what they didn't do now know. Indulge me, and let me remember—if only for a little while—how much fun I had, and still have, on the field, playing ball. I didn't want to get back at anyone. And today, thanks to my mom and dad, who are looking down from above, God has returned to me everything I lost back then, and then some. I can't ask God for anything else. And I don't have anything else to say about what happened, at least not for now.

The guy who was still at my side back then was Signorini, Fernando "El Ciego" Signorini. He would go with me to Mexico along with Salvatore Carmando, who was Napoli's masseuse—another phenomenon. The two of them were working for me. It wouldn't cost the Argentine team a red cent, and they wouldn't meddle in the team's affairs. But both were key to my physical condition, and I didn't want to leave anything to chance, I mean nothing at all. That's why Claudia and my family stayed behind. The only ones who came were my dad, don Diego, and my father-in-law at the time, Coco, who would become the team's official barbecue grill master. Nobody else.

THE TEAM, NOT THE TALK

We couldn't believe it when we got to the training camp. It was a whorehouse with no whores! I mean, with all due respect for the people who worked there and gratitude for the warm welcome they gave us, we had to take care of everything ourselves—even change the lightbulbs—because construction was not finished on all the rooms. I mean it. Pachamé had to take over like a master builder. The rooms were small, with exposed brick, a lightbulb hanging down from the ceiling, and two cots. That's it. There weren't enough rooms for everyone (they had prepared for sixteen players and there were twenty-two of us plus the coaching staff). So we had to add a room in a shed area, with a cardboard partition. That's where Valdano and Trobbiani stayed. They called it "the island" because it was far away from the rest. "El Tata" Brown was there too—he had to put up with "El Kaiser," though he ended up earning his position on the team—as well as "El Cabezón" Ruggeri and Almirón.

The rooms had numbers: 12, 14, 15, 16, and 17. There was no 13, out of superstition. Bilardo liked the whole situation because he liked seeing players suffer. I mean, I could take it, we all could, but really—come on! He had taken fourteen of the guys to train at high altitude in Tilcara before the cup. Was this really necessary? To justify what exactly? They still claim that those guys made a pledge at a church while they were in Tilcara that they would return if we won the World Cup, and since they didn't keep their word, we have never been world champions again. Come on—that's bullshit!

Get real! When I think about it now, years later, I think Bilardo did things like that because he knew he would be blamed because we were a mess on the field and he had to explain it somehow. We had not yet started to play the game the way it should be played. I mean it when I say it looked like we would be the worst team at the cup that year.

That's why I say today that more credit should go to the players out there on the field and less to the coach's tactics. It was the team, not the talk. Some thirty years later, that seems fair.

So we set up there before anyone else and started to live the World Cup experience more intensely than anyone else. I shared a room with Pedrito Pasculli; it was room number 6, but if it were today, I would ask for number 10. It was the same as all the others, with two cots, exposed brick wall, and so on. At first there was nothing on the walls, but then Pedrito and I started putting up photos, from Our Lady of Luján to the actress Valeria Lynch—a little of everything.

Clausen and Burru, who knew each other from the Independiente team, roomed together, as did Nery and "El Vasco" Olarticoechea. Bocha was with "El Gringo" Giusti (they were both from Independiente too). Claudio "El Bichi" Borghi, who was just a kid, was with Cuciuffo—a great player from Córdoba province. What a pity what happened to him, the hunting accident in 2004; I remember he was like a little kid, just thrilled to be at the cup. "El Mago" Garré was with Zelada, a great goalie—Mexico was like home court for him because he played there. Tapia with Enrique. "El Loco" Islas who, though just a kid too, had a lot of character, roomed with "Checho" Batista.

Moschella, Rubén Moschella, who took care of all the administrative tasks, roomed with Molina, one of the team's masseuses. I say "one of them" because I had taken Carmando; Salvatore was in a tiny room he shared with Roberto Mariani—who was one of Bilardo's assistants—"El Ciego" Signorini, and Miguel di Lorenzo, better known as El Loco Galíndez. Oh my God, you should have seen that room! I used to say that they slept so close together they had the same dreams.

Galíndez was a masseuse too, but he wore a thousand hats. He not only helped the kit man but was also the team's comedian, so he was exhausted by the end of the day. Every night he would head to his room and flop onto his cot as if it was a swimming pool. I mean, he would collapse. One day, we loosened the screws on the bed's legs and gathered at a window to see if he would throw himself in as usual. And he did! Galíndez went down—plop!—and the mattress hit the floor. He wanted to kill us when he saw us spying through the window. That wasn't the only practical joke we pulled. Just as we didn't hold back and said everything we had to say outright, we also fooled around like a bunch of kids. I mean, there wasn't a lot to do except train. There were no cell phones back then, man! I mean, that whole mess with Passarella was because he was using the only phone line at the camp.

The other thing we did was read the Mexican sports papers—*Esto, Ovaciones, La Afición*—and wait for *El Gráfico*, the Argentine sports magazine, to get there. No computers or anything like that! The first one up in the morning was always Trobbiani. What a pain in the ass! At seven thirty in the morning he was out on the field. I would love to go and have a few matés in the kit room, with Tito Benrós and El Loco Galíndez. They live and breathe soccer in the kit rooms; those guys work their asses off, getting to the field four hours before you and leaving four hours after.

THE TEAM DIET? CARMANDO'S PASTAS AND MY OLD MAN'S BARBECUES

As I have said a number of times, I don't like life in training camps. But this time it wasn't so stifling because we did a lot of things we players wanted to. We took that trip to Colombia but came back early because we wanted to experience the altitude firsthand. The rooms were an issue, but I thought the fields would be great for training. The premises were enormous— almost ten acres—and surrounded by a forest. It was like forty minutes from downtown Mexico City, but Azteca stadium was just five minutes away, which was really fantastic. The truth is, we ended up adapting to everything, and it became like a second home. "El Zurdo" López, who had been my coach at Argentinos Juniors and was the director of Club América, would come and go. He's a great guy, and was always doing what he could to help out.

Every so often Bilardo would organize games against local clubs and youth teams. It was a menace, because sometimes the kids would play to kill. But he wanted us to train, to keep running, and to get used to the goddamn altitude once and for all. Training helped us breathe better, so we were all up for it. Our chests were heaving, and we wanted to get them heaving even more, so when it came time for the games in the cup, under the noonday sun, we wouldn't even feel it. I went up to Checho Batista and he said to me, "I can't take it. I just can't . . ."

"Me neither, but come on, keep going . . ."

We held each other by the arm and pushed each other ahead.

"Hold on, Maradona, one sec," he said.

"Come on, let's go, Checho. We can do it. Come on."

I really wanted to train hard, but Bilardo wouldn't let us. He would tell us to stop. Sometimes he would organize those games at midday and then a practice session in the afternoon. But he really wanted us to rest up. And I had no interest in resting: it was one of many differences between us.

One day, I went up to the kit man Tito Benrós and said, "Gimme a ball. We're going to play."

"But, Diego, I can't. Bilardo will kill me."

"Stop screwing around and gimme a ball or I'll kill you."

I would never have laid a finger on Tito. He was a great

guy. But Bilardo had him at his beck and call. Anyway, he gave me the ball and, a little while later, a bunch of us—Tito included—were playing a pickup game in a meadow in the back, behind the fields.

I would often go up to "El Profe" Echevarría and say, "Listen, Bochini, Almirón, and so-and-so look slow to me—and I feel slow myself. Out behind the rooms there's another field. Don't say a word to Bilardo, but grab some of those cones because we're going back there. Do some zigzag drills, a long sprint, another zigzag drill, ten laps, two times around, ten laps . . . That's it."

"That's just why I love you so much, Diego. Let's go . . . I want to train you guys, but Carlos doesn't want me to," he would explain.

A monument—and a big one—should be built to Echevarría. He was a genius, and he also kept Bilardo calm. He would come up to my bed and whisper to me, "Are you going to train today? Or does your ankle hurt?"

"It hurts a little," I'd say.

And he would say, "Take it easy, then. I'll take the mares out into the pasture first, and then you join in later, nice and easy."

"El Profe" knew just what to do. Great guy.

Madero, "Doc" Eduardo Madero, was another story. I'm still not sure what he went to Mexico for. He would talk to the journalists about all these great meals we were eating: cream of pea soup, ravioli with cream and walnut sauce, brisket with noisette potatoes, flan with cream, vermicelli *aglio e olio*, chicken à la Portugaise—some carbohydrates here, some other stuff over there . . .

The only meals I remember are the ones "El Loco" Oliva gave me. He knew what he was talking about, and I had blind faith in him. They may tell you about one menu or another, but the truth is Julito Onieva, the cook, was amazing. Still, what I remember most when it comes to food were Carmando's pastas, which he would serve on these enormous platters whenever we asked for them, and my old man's barbecues twice a week.

I also remember going to Eduardo Cremasco's restaurant, Mi Viejo, which became a classic for us. "El Cabezón" Cremasco had been a teammate of Bilardo's at Estudiantes. He had been living in Mexico for some time, and he was the guy who got us the meat for the barbecues. He was also involved in a lot of the team rituals and superstitions. We had a thousand of them. For example, after every game we would go eat at his restaurant, which was in Polanco, a fancy neighborhood in Mexico City. Another ritual was to go to the Perisur mall before games. It was enormous and had four large department stores: Liverpool, El Palacio de Hierro, Sears, and Sanborns. The team went to Sanborns the first time. I say "the team" because I didn't go along; my knee was hurting and I was afraid something would happen. I had to be careful—it might have been easy going at the beginning of the cup, but I knew things would get tricky as it progressed.

One thing we would always do—no matter how many of us there were—was down a few hot dogs, which were as stiff as rolling pins, and get an ice cream at Helen's. We would even put on their foam hats—it may have been free advertising for them, but it helped us.

Then there was the whole thing with the bus, which we would take everywhere because everything was pretty close to the camp. We would take the bus to Olímpico stadium, for example, where we played the first game. I am not talking about some luxury bus here. It was more like a van, really. And that's the way it was with everything. We were always goofing off. I would always say, "See you later," when I left the training camp to make it clear that I would be coming back. "El Profe" Echevarría would stand in the middle of the aisle before we would pull out. "Are we all here?" he would ask, even though he knew that we were.

The last guy to get on the bus was Pachamé. He would sit with Bilardo in the first row. And we troublemakers would sit smack-dab in the middle and start in with our chants and songs, and it would go downhill from there. It was Tapia, Islas, Zelada, Almirón, "El Vasco" Olarticoechea, but even Mariani would get in on it sometimes. And driving in front of us would be two motorcycles, as an escort, which Jesús and Tobías were always driving. They had been with us since day one, when we landed, almost a month before the first game. Whether we went to Olímpico or to Azteca stadium, superstition said it always had to take us exactly as long as it had taken the first time, even if that meant speeding like a bullet or parking somewhere to kill time.

Every time we arrived at a stadium, we had to do interviews with the same reporters who had interviewed us at the first game, "El Ruso" Ramenzoni and Tití Fernández. It was crazy, the first time in history that the players went looking for the reporters to interview them. We always had to play the same songs too, of course: Bonnie Tyler's ballad "Total Eclipse of the Heart" and the Sergio Denis tune "Gigante chiquito," which made me cry like a baby; the theme from *Rocky*—my favorite—would make me feel stronger than Dal

Monte's training sessions. If you didn't hit the field ready to rip the other team to shreds after listening to that—plus all the rage and enthusiasm we had inside—then you were made of stone and not fit for the team.

THE FAVORITES NEVER WIN

The only thing we needed to get out of the first game was a win. To win no matter what. They had lit into us so hard before we made it to the cup that to lose against a team of guys that looked like robots, one just like the next, would be fatal. But in my mind I knew it was better not to be the favorites—the favorites never win.

And I'm sure a lot of Argentines didn't believe in us. They didn't understand the lineup. And, truth be told, we didn't either.

Two days before the game against South Korea we didn't know if we were going in with two stoppers or two fullbacks, if Cuciuffo or Clausen or Garré was going to play. We didn't know basic stuff like that! And then there was the whole Passarella issue, which was the big question until right before the game.

Two days before the first game, Bilardo had come up with a lineup at a forty-five-minute practice when Passarella was still around. But Passarella already had the runs by then—or at least he said he did. The team was Pumpido as goalie; Clausen as right fullback; Passarella and Ruggeri as stoppers; Garré as left fullback; Giusti, Batista, Burruchaga, and me at midfield; and Valdano and Pasculli as forwards.

I would love someone to tell me, here and now, what, if anything, that lineup had to do with the one we ended up using? But that's part of this story, of the true story. Because if "El Vasco" Olarticoechea, who was not even in the lineup at the beginning, hadn't back-headed the ball in that match against the English, we'd have nothing to talk about. They go on and on about Bilardo's tactics, but he didn't realize that when Barnes came in, he juked us twice on the same side. Bilardo didn't do anything about it. Why doesn't anyone say that he messed up—can you tell me that? But I'm getting all worked up and there is still a while to go before that game.

All I'm saying is that I'm tired of hearing that the big winner of the '86 World Cup was Bilardo. Bilardo, my ass! The winners of the '86 World Cup were the players, one and all, because we put up with all of Bilardo's bullshit. Because what Bilardo likes is to see a player suffer. And that idea is outdated, stuck in the past.

And speaking of time, Passarella's was just about up.

We had to wait until the day of the game to find out. We left the training camp at ten in the morning because Olímpico stadium wasn't far away. And ten minutes before, they told us that "El Kaiser"—the former great captain—wasn't going to play.

"You'll go in for him," Bilardo told "El Tata" Brown, who wasn't even a starter for any professional club. He was a sub for Deportivo Español.

I remember that all hell broke loose, and how scared we all were because we all thought our game would be lost without Passarella, and nobody imagined how much "El Tata" Brown could deliver. Well, not nobody. My teammates and I had blind faith in him. We knew that he would give his life for the Argentine jersey. He was one of Bilardo's boys, but he didn't give a shit about the whole Bilardo-versus-Menotti thing. He was such a humble guy that, during that awful tour we did in Colombia before the cup, he had stood staring like a little boy at a Rolex in the duty-free shop.

"Get it," I told him.

"I can't, Diego," he said.

When we got back to the camp in Mexico, I gave him the watch. I had bought it for him as a present. I had a gut feeling that this guy was going to give us a hand to win at the World Cup.

But we had a game—a number of games—before that. First off, the opening game. Just think what they would have said if we couldn't beat a bunch of Koreans! We didn't even know their names, and Bilardo even less so. He had killed us with all his videos, but he didn't know who was who.

What we didn't imagine was that the South Koreans were going to sock it to us as much as our detractors. Or even more. What we did know was that we could win the game with aerial play, no matter what changes Bilardo made at practices. And aerial play would work because, well, the Koreans were short. Easy as pie. And we had to get over the breathlessness because of the altitude, because the Koreans were tough physically. We had to outrun them. And we had trained for that.

As soon as we hit the field at Olímpico stadium in Mexico City on Monday, June 2, the day of the game, we realized that we were going to have a lot of Mexicans rooting against us. Not all of them, but some. But that made sense: they always root for the underdog. I don't think it was because they were anti-Argentine or anything.

But they knew we were capable of scoring four goals against the Koreans. It did piss me off when, later, they cheered the German goals—but that was much later. There must have been some three thousand Argentines in the bleachers who shouted as much as they could, a good many Koreans who made quite a ruckus, but all together there were forty thousand people there and all of them—except for the little group who, for one reason or other, had faith in us—were dead against us! But that was nothing new. In fact, it was all the better for us. We were so used to adversity that it just made us stronger.

THE FIRST GOAL AT THE WORLD CUP

I'll never forget the first lineup, the one that took that first step: Pumpido; Clausen, Brown, Ruggeri and Garré; Giusti, Batista, Burruchaga, and me; Pasculli and Valdano.

Thirty seconds in—just thirty seconds—I got kicked for the first time. The player was named Kim, I think, and he got me from behind. Sánchez Arminio, the Spanish ref, didn't say a thing. Not a peep. And there was, by that time, plenty of talk about fair play in soccer. President of FIFA and the former water polo player João Havelange had been going on and on all week: "Reward skill, punish violence." Nice phrase for a bumper sticker, but not what we saw on the field.

I got back on my feet, cool as a cucumber, and lined the ball up for a free kick. That was exactly what we needed: free kicks, either close to the penalty area or not so close but—like this one—would help us kick high balls. For this one, we tried that. I kicked it to the right, and even though Valdano couldn't get control of the ball we were heading in the right direction. Was this a planned play? You bet, planned by us, by the players. We were the ones planning the plays, man!

I got fouled eleven times. Eleven! I'm not sure if that's a lot or a little, but they were all really rough. Brutal.

Thirty years have passed, but when I watched the footage of the game for the first time, it still hurt. One of them spiked me so hard that it went right through my sock and my bandage—and the bandages I wore, above my socks, were like casts. I would always wrap the bandages the same way. Carmando not only gave me massages but also wrapped me up. It was a ritual in the locker room. It gave me a sense of security. First, I would put my shin guards on good and tight, then my socks, which I would pull up above the knee. And only then would Carmando come over and put the bandages on with his magic hands. It was like a cast—I swear to God.

I wore the same cleats, the Puma Kings, for the whole cup. I had taken five pairs with me to Mexico and had broken them in so much they felt like part of my foot. I would put on all five pairs the nights before the games, but I would always end up wearing the same ones—they fit me like a glove. And the spikes—high in the back and lower in the front—were basic. I wouldn't say that I was playing in high heels, but I have recommended that difference in spike length to a number of players and many have started using shoes like that for the traction. The spikes in the back give you more support so you can stop suddenly.

But no matter how many bandages I wore or how good my cleats were, I was still getting kicked.

One of those fouls led to the free kick that was our first goal. It's the foul in that famous shot: the guy is going straight for my right knee and I am screaming in pain. Because it really killed! When I watched the game, I realized one thing: the guy, whose name was Park—even though he was not at all amusing, I'll tell you—kicked me at the three-minute mark, and I did the free kick at the five-minute mark. That means I had only two minutes to recover. And the kick was no bullshit. But the idiot ref didn't say anything, let alone give him a yellow card!

I took the free kick myself, but I couldn't get the ball up in the air. I don't know if I lacked precision because I was still hurting or what, but the ball bounced off the wall and right onto my head. Without giving it a thought, I passed it to Valdano on my right—just like the previous play, the first one in the game. Jorge was there with time to spare and crossed the ball to the other side of the goalpost. It went in between the goalie, who was named Ho, and Pasculli, who had bolted right down the middle in case Valdano wanted to pass it there. Ho! It was just what we all shouted out. It was the first goal in the World Cup, so it really mattered.

WHAT ABOUT FAIR PLAY, ANYWAY?

Their coach had said that I was just another player, and so he wasn't going to have a guy mark me. And, in fact, he was right: I was just another player. And he didn't lie when he said he wasn't going to assign someone to mark me. What he did was send the whole team out to light into me. They would take turns at it, and that was about all they would do. They started playing more defensively, which made sense since they were behind, one to nothing. But we kept up the attack. Before the ten-minute mark, we had two chances at a goal, once with Clausen and once with Burruchaga.

And we were so worried about our lungs burning that when I passed the ball to Burruchaga, who landed an amazing kick that hit the goalpost, we just went right on playing, totally unfazed. We didn't want to waste any energy on that.

Before we were twenty minutes in, Kim came after me again, more or less in the same place as that first foul. This time, though, I calculated the free kick better. Pasculli faked them out by going right over the ball. I kicked it, and it went straight to Ruggeri, who drove it into Ho's net. No more screwing around. We were winning, two to nothing. End of story. That was just what we needed. I was happy because we had played better in the first half hour than we had during the whole tour before the cup. Nice and easy, no problem. We were beat up, it's true. The Koreans would light into you for the fun of it. Their number 10—my number, of all numbers— brought me down at midfield, far from where the action was, and then gave me a hand to help me up. I was feeling so good that I accepted all apologies.

We played well, really well, for the first twenty-five minutes. Then we let up a little. I wasn't thrilled by the idea, but it did make some sense. It was too hot, it was the first game, and we were up against a team that couldn't do us any real harm. And I understood that if I kept protesting about every last thing, they would kick me out of the game. From then on, we controlled the ball a lot but it was harder for us to do any real damage. They were doing us plenty of damage, though, but not by getting near to scoring. I don't think that Nery, our goalie, touched the ball once that whole first half. And the game became so boring that even the Argentine fans in the stadium stood up in the human wave—a custom we had never seen before the cup.

In the middle of all this—that is, in the middle of nothing— Clausen passed me the ball from the side; we were at midfield, on our side of the field but only slightly, and number 17 on their team came at me from behind like nothing I'd ever seen before. He kicked me in such a weird way that I ended up, inexplicably, cut right behind my knee. I showed the guys afterward, and they couldn't believe it either. And do you know who came to help me up with a pat on the back, as if nothing had happened? That's right, that son of a bitch Sánchez Arminio, the referee.

The left fullback was the guy who kicked me, and he did it again just a little while later, right before halftime. The guy came to get me at midfield, near the central circle. I saw him coming and nutmegged the ball, using the outside of my left foot. The ball went through, but that son of a bitch kept his arm up, and it rammed into my jaw. It wasn't a kick: it was a punch—bam!—a clean blow. That was when the Spaniard gave him a yellow card. It took him forty-four minutes to pull one out! The card went to number 17, the bastard. I didn't even know his name. The guy even complained about getting the card.

But the guy's name, it turned out, was Huh Jung-Moo, and wouldn't you know that I ran into him many years later at the 2010 World Cup in South Africa when he was coaching the South Korean team. The stubborn bastard said he had nothing to apologize for: if he had done something wrong, they would have had to throw him out of the game. "I didn't hit you on purpose. If I had, the referee would have thrown me out of the game. But I didn't even get a warning that game," he said. He also said that '86 was the first time they had qualified for a World Cup in thirty-two years, which is why they were a bit jumpy. Jumpy? They were going a hundred miles an hour!

"I don't care what Maradona says. It's pointless to talk about something that happened over twenty years ago," he said. I didn't contradict him because it wasn't worth it, though

I did say, in more general terms, that if there are four kids who carry out the yellow fair-play flag before each game, there should be fair play on the field. We have to defend the star players and the referees have to understand what "fair play" really means. If people go out there to watch a soccer game, the players shouldn't have to put up with so much trouble.

Messi had a better time playing against the players Huh Jung-Moo coached than I had playing against his teammates and him.

One minute into the second half, I broke past the defense on the right side of the field, dodging the kicks of two of their guys, and kicked it center with my right foot. Pedrito Pasculli ran right past the goalie, and then Valdano came up on the other side and pushed the ball in. All set. Three to nothing. Lay back but be careful. We had to stay in good shape and watch our legs, making sure nobody on the team got hurt.

The other thing we had to be careful about was the altitude. That's why you can tell that we were taking things nice and easy, no problem. You could most definitely feel those eighty-five hundred feet, and though we were always on the attack, we kept losing possession of the ball. It's a good thing the Koreans didn't know what to do with the ball, because we served it to them on a platter on more than one occasion. They couldn't do us any harm, even though they did score one goal near the end. But we had them completely under control. I teased the shit out of poor Pumpido, the goalie! The guy had kicked it way the hell in there, and I yelled at him, "It's okay, Nery, you almost got that one!"

We had beaten them through aerial play, just like we had planned: centering the ball any chance we got, because somebody would be there to score. I kept kicking it over to Valdano from the left. But there were still some things that didn't go all that smoothly. They would come at us from the sides, and we were still using our classic lineup with Clausen on the right and Garré on the left. At the beginning of the cup, Clausen was in amazing shape, but he could never adjust to the altitude—he was one of the guys who had the most trouble with it. We had yet to see the famous wingbacks Bilardo had bragged about.

Burruchaga was settling in nicely, but Bilardo would drive him nuts. It's awful when a coach starts screaming at you and you feel cornered. "Tell him to quit yelling at me, Diego," Burru would say to me. So I went over to him and said, "Easy does it, Carlos, easy does it." And he at least motioned that he would lay off. "Checho" Batista also had trouble that first game. The altitude was no joke, and Bilardo was screaming at him all the time too. In the end, he took him out and put "El Vasco" Olarticoechea in, which he would do on a number of occasions. The other substitution was when Tapia went in for Pasculli.

The one who nailed it was "El Tata" Brown, who made everyone forget all about Passarella and worked great with "El Cabezón" Ruggeri. I still believe that Passarella didn't play because he didn't want to. Knowing him, knowing his good side—which was his commitment, his guts—he could have played. But he made the decision he made, and it didn't work out for him. Because El Tata did great and, in that first game, he earned his position. Nobody was going to take it away from him after that.

I ended that game in a fight with Valdano—I can't remember why. But we didn't speak to each other for like four days afterward. Not until he came to my room and we patched things up. We were both being really petty. A number of guys threatened to go back to Buenos Aires: Enrique, for instance, even though he had balls the size of the whole training camp; "El Loco" Islas, who was just a kid but couldn't stand being a sub; and "El Checho" Batista, who was realizing that he would be the first one to be benched . . . Really petty.

STICK UP FOR THE GOOD GUYS

Italy and Bulgaria—who were our real rivals in the group—had started the cup with an awful game that ended in a one-to-one tie. I saw how slow and heavy they were on the field, and I thought of Professor Dal Monte. It's a good thing that Bearzot didn't want him to give them a hand! I knew a bunch of guys on the team, and it wouldn't be long before I'd come up against them. I was really eager for the match against Italy.

And the French, with that heartless turkey Platini, who hardly touched the ball, had just barely beaten Canada, one to nothing; Canada caused them much more trouble than South Korea had caused us. Papin scored near the end of the game. I liked the fact that the big-name players on all the teams were not delivering as expected. It was only the opening match, but something I have always said—and still say— was bearing out: a World Cup is a World Cup, and there's nothing like it. It stands out from the rest.

And you can see which players stand out too: the real greats.

In the opening game, Brazil beat Spain with a goal by Sócrates, but as usual, it was largely luck: a kick by Platini hit the crossbar and bounced in the net, but they disqualified it. A big controversy broke out, but Brazil got the points, though

Zico was on the bench, it's true. I didn't say a word, but my most direct rivals were barely playing. Rummenigge played a little, to help West Germany tie Uruguay. But not much else. The Soviet team gave the Hungarians the run around, scoring six goals. They were great, with Dasayev as goalie and Belanov upfield. And the Danes proved that they were lethal on offense: Elkjaer Larsen came in from Italy, where he played for Verona, in amazing shape and he scored in the opening match. And I saw something in the Belgian team, even though they lost to the Mexicans with Hugo Sánchez.

I looked at us more than at the others, though I did keep my eye on them. And for us, with all the hard times we had faced, the opening had been amazing. That's why, after that game—which was at midday—we went back to the training camp but we didn't have dinner there. We all went to "El Cabezón" Cremasco's restaurant. I mean, we had earned ourselves a nice Argentine steak, a few tangos sung by "El Zurdo" López, and Galíndez's impersonations—I take it back, *that* we did not deserve. But there we were.

Suddenly, at the end of dinner, some Argentines at other tables started chanting, "We're gonna win it! We're gonna win it . . . !"

I looked at them, as did the rest of the guys, and listened to them, and I couldn't believe it. "So now we're going to win the whole thing?" I wondered. They flipped like flapjacks . . .

The dinner also gave us a chance to go over the game. The Koreans should have been given five cards. Five, at least! They kicked the shit out of us and they only got one card at the end of the first period. They would dive right into me and then turn around and apologize. Unbelievable.

Asians used to be more violent and clever players. Their

game has changed a lot. Asian soccer has, I think, developed more than African soccer, which is sort of stuck in a rut.

But those kicks were good for something. Because today if they so much as touch Messi, or Neymar, or Ronaldo, it's a yellow card. Or even a red card. And that's how it should be! That's what the FIFA should do: defend skill, defend the good guys. They should deal with violence and a few other things too. Can someone please tell me how they could put Ibrahimović up against Cristiano for the qualifications of the last World Cup, for example? Ibrahimović was eliminated, but they both should have been there!

You have to stick up for good guys on and off the field— even though no one ever stood up for me.

CHAPTER 4

Mamma Mia

ARGENTINA 1, ITALY 1
—Puebla, Thursday, June 5

Thanks to the curl I put on the ball, I make five out of every ten shots on goal. Only five, just half. What I mean is that if I do it again, if I kick the ball in the exact same way, half the time I will be standing there cursing because I missed it and half the time I will be screaming my head off, ecstatic about the goal I just scored. I am talking about me—not a player better or worse than myself. That's what would happen to me.

I'm really talking about the goal I scored against Italy in the third game of the World Cup. I would put that goal right up there in ranking the best goals scored over the course of my career. Because of how I screwed Scirea and the way I scored it—how I kicked it in—right past Galli and into the other side of the net. For technical and historical reasons, it is one of the best goals of my life. And one of the goals I celebrated the most as well.

OF COURSE IT WAS A SPECIAL GAME

I want to make myself perfectly clear, because seeing it is one thing, telling it another, but doing it—that's indescribable! Check out how I kick the ball, with the inside of my left foot. The ball should have gone off to the right, parallel to the end line, like a center that a winger kicks to reach a forward, but no! It went left. The ball went between the sweeper and the goalie, who rushed out. It went right in the other side of the net.

An amazing goal. Just amazing . . . Few like it.

Later Galli, the goalie, was a teammate of mine at Napoli. "Diego, I swear on my child that the ball sailed six feet past me," he would tell me every single day. And he would go on and on, as if I were a priest and he were confessing or apologizing. "People say, 'Why didn't you grab it?' Don't you think I would have if I could have? The ball changed course, just like that, when it was within reach. And then it was behind me, as if the wind had swept it in. It was like you didn't kick it at all but hit it with a racket, like a tennis player playing the net."

I loved that comparison; I love tennis.

They all blame him for the goal because in all the photos he looks like a fool, his hand stretched out like that. It looks like the ball is just a few inches—not a yard—away. But who's to blame? Scirea. One hundred percent. Because if Scirea had just touched the ball, it was Galli's ball. Galli's ball, right? And back then you could still do a back-pass to the goalie.

That's why, to my mind, Scirea's the only one to blame for that goal I scored against Italy. He was an exceptional sweeper, who was used to playing for Juve—he rarely needed to boot the ball or anything like that. He had great timing. But what he didn't know was that I had studied him good. When he faked to the left, he would go right; when a high ball was coming in and it looked as if he was going to boot it, he would do a chest trap.

And in that play, when the ball bounced and Scirea faked as if he was going to boot it right, I beat him to it because I knew he wasn't really going to do it. And before the ball hit the ground and he could pull back his right leg to kick, I put my foot down just so, which he had no way of expecting, and Galli couldn't reach it.

Scirea's only option would have been to back-pass it to Galli. It wouldn't have been an own goal, because Galli was facing him. Anyway, it was my goal. But that's the strange thing, what I was talking about before: only five of ten balls pass right between two opposing players, parallel to the end line. And, while the two of them end up looking like fools in the photo—bam!—it goes in the other side of the net.

I was so happy that I went running off the field, jumping over the advertising board on the perimeter as if it were a traffic cone. There is no way I can jump like that anymore; many believe I went over to *that* advertisement because it was prearranged that I would celebrate over there. If that were the case, I still need to get paid, because no one clued me in.

The goal was sweet and the game special. I'd been playing in Italy for almost two seasons—not long, really—but I already knew everybody. And they knew me. It was special. I knew that I had gone to play in a country that lives and breathes soccer. In a city, Naples, where soccer is life itself.

When I arrived, they asked me to beat Juve, to beat Milan, to beat Inter. And then that wasn't enough. They also wanted a championship.

Of course the game against Italy was special. But, truth be told, back then the pressure wasn't all that bad. It wasn't as bad as when we played them four years later, in '90, on their home field, which was also my home field, because the game was in Naples. It was do or die that time. That was different. The Italians wanted to murder me. The headline of the *La Gazzetta dello Sport* read "Maradona è il Diavolo" ("Maradona Is the Devil"). That's how it was four years later. But things were different in '86. The Italians even found it kind of amusing. I mean, until then I had never snatched a championship away from any of the big teams, so they still liked me.

I WASN'T YET "IL DIAVOLO"

Almost exactly two years before, in July of '84, Naples made a good impression on me. A lot of things about that city reminded me of my origins, and also of La Boca, where I played in Argentina. It was easy to feel at home there, even though it was a crazy town. What I didn't know was that regardless of the thousands and thousands of fans—as if it were a great team, because it was great in its way—Napoli was, in soccer terms, closer to the second division than to a championship.

What it was, was a second-division team playing against a third-division team for the Supercoppa, a team that ended up downfield trying to keep the other team from scoring. That happened to me when I first started playing with them, for real. I knew I was going to suffer—a lot—but I also knew that the harder something is, the more I like it. The way it was with the Argentine team. The less faith they had in me or in us, the angrier I was and the harder I played.

I think that's why I felt at home at Napoli from the get-go. It wasn't until after I had signed the contract that I found out that the team was on the verge of being relegated to a lower division, that it had sneaked by the last season by just one point! But I would have signed even had I known. I was as crazy as they were. I felt that they loved me, that they really and truly loved me. There had been hunger strikes and people had chained themselves to the fence at San Paolo stadium, begging me to come. How could I let them down? Besides, the fight would do me good.

I did know that to play in Italy, to play against the Italian defensive players, I was going to have to train differently. In Spain they would kick you in the tongue if they got a chance; they would hack at you and elbow you good, but they were not as clever when it came to marking. They were more violent and also more direct. The Italians, on the other hand, were experts. Beyond what had happened to me with Claudio Gentile at the World Cup in Spain, most of them were master markers. They trained for that. Nowadays there are so few defensive players in Italy that they have to nationalize players from other countries, but in those years they had more than they knew what to do with. This is why I brought "El Ciego" Fernando Signorini over from Spain with me. He knew a lot about training and, along with Dr. Oliva, he had been crucial to my recovery from my injury. I had to be in great shape physically to handle what was coming my way. In all respects.

That's why I say that playing for Napoli was the best preparation imaginable for the World Cup in Mexico. The very best. First off, because they made me feel important, because they made me feel necessary—which was no longer the case at Barcelona. Second, because I had to be in tip-top shape to get around guys who were supposedly better than me—than us—and definitely better than the Spanish players when it came to marking. And, third, because it prepared me to have everyone and everything against me.

And, hell, you really felt that in Napoli: everyone and everything against us. I remember my official debut against Verona, with the Danish player Elkjaer Larsen and the German player Hans-Peter Briegel. The German player was so intimidating he could take me off the field with just a glance. He was a monster physically! But even worse were the guys who would hold up banners saying, "Welcome to Italy." That whole battle between the North and the South made me stronger and gave me a chance to do what I like best: fight for a cause. And if it's the cause of the poor, all the better.

It wasn't easy, not at all. It never has been for me. I'm always fighting against something. The thing is, at the end of the first round in that first season, Napoli had nine points. I was dying of shame when I came back to Buenos Aires for Christmas. But I knew it was an opportunity, a great opportunity. And I wasn't going to let it go by. When I got back, we got more points than that Verona team, the team of millionaires—that oh-so-European club. We got twenty-four points and they got twenty-two. They won the championship, it's true, but we let them know what we were there for. I scored fourteen goals, almost as many as that kid Platini. The Italian league had a lot of big deal players at the time. Every team had one or two: Platini at Juve, Rummenigge at Inter,

Laudrup at Lazio, Zico at Udinese, Sócrates and Passarella at Fiorentina, and Falcão and Toninho Cerezo at Roma. What a bunch of guys. What better way to get ready to fight it out in Mexico?

Still, I needed to play at a higher level—for me, for the Argentine team, and for them, for Napoli. I had to help the Neapolitans fight the rest of Italy, especially the more powerful teams from the North, teams like Juve, Inter, and Milan, which is why I threatened Ferlaino with leaving if he didn't bring in reinforcements for the '85–'86 season, the one right before the World Cup. That was how Alessandro Renica was brought in from Sampdoria; Claudio Garella, the goalie for the championship Verona team, who would block shots with his feet, but block them all the same; and, mostly, Bruno Giordano, from Lazio. I loved Giordano because, with all the troubles he had had, he seemed like a perfect fit with Napoli.

Nobody wanted to go to Napoli because of the camorra (the local mafia), because of the city itself and everything that was going on there. But Giordano was experienced, real experienced. He had been involved in the Totonero match-fixing scandal, and at Lazio he played everywhere—right, left, center. I wanted him by my side, and I went to get him myself. He said yes right away. It cost three million dollars and made Ferlaino cry, but it was worth it. I didn't have to lead the team by myself. He would stick a few yards behind me as I moved upfield; I scored eleven goals and he scored twelve. We really took Napoli up there. We ended in third place, within six points of Juve, the team that won the championship, and we qualified for the UEFA Cup. The Neapolitans couldn't believe it, but I could.

I'm going to say it again: what better way to get ready for

a World Cup than that? We played against the best, and I had learned a ton out on the field: I knew how to break loose, not to hold back. And I could do all that when they treated us like dirt.

I mean, I was up against the same stuff at Napoli as I was on the Argentine team. And my mind was already in the World Cup. What I was doing was good for Napoli and for the Argentine team.

The coach by then was Bianchi, Ottavio Bianchi. But we players were our own coach. I didn't like him from the get-go.

So that was where I was coming from when I reached the cup—I was used to a lot of stuff, especially fighting when things were rough. The truth is, before Mexico '86, Platini was the big winner, the guy who won all the titles, and I was the *giocoliere*, the juggler, the one who did the nutmegs, the rabonas, the rainbow kicks, but no victory laps or titles for me.

Screw that! What I wanted was to win. To win it all and beat everyone—anyone who stood in my way. And that's how it would turn out: I would fight and fight until finally I managed to topple the Platini myth.

JUST ONE TV FOR EVERYONE

There's wasn't a lot to do at the training camp. Just one TV for everyone, and it was in the dining hall, for watching the games. Then there were the Mexican sports papers like *Esto*, *Ovación*, and *La Afición*. And once a week—long after it came out in Argentina—*El Gráfico* would arrive. I remember one issue pissed me off. It had an interview with Platini—of all guys—and the headline said, "A Pleasure to Interview Plat-ini." How could it possibly be a pleasure to interview that heartless French turkey? I lost it. It still drives me nuts. And, in the same issue, an article on Pelé. It was like they were doing it on purpose—maybe to piss me off or to get me riled up.

And what did Pelé have to say? When I reread it, it makes me want to hit the field to show him again what I already had. He said, "This is Diego's last real chance to show that he is the best in the world. I don't think he has won enough tro-phies so far to say without a doubt that he is number one. He was a disaster in Spain—irritable, getting kicked out of games; he spent the whole time down on the ground pretend-ing to have been fouled. That's why I don't think he is the best. In fact, Platini, Zico, and Rummenigge are not only as good as he is, but even a little better. When Platini gets knocked down, he stands back up and keeps right on playing. Mara-dona stays where he is and looks over at the ref. I know that it hurts when they knock you down, but once you reach a cer-tain level you have to have the class to dodge the blows and to know how to handle things in a pinch."

It would take a few more games or, actually, a few more years to show Pelé and Platini who was who.

AGAINST ITALY, WE STARTED BELIEVING IN OURSELVES

That afternoon in Puebla, I didn't have to deal with Platini. Instead, I had to deal with the Italian team and coaching staff—guys I got along with.

Some of them were opponents in that North-South

struggle. There was only one teammate of mine on the Italian team—plus a guy who had played for a smaller club but would later join Napoli.

The coach, Enzo Bearzot, had my teammate mark me. I don't know if he thought he could outplay me because he knew me, but the truth is I was three notches above Salva, Salvatore Bagni—that was the guy. He also wore the number 10 jersey, but for Italy! But he wasn't a playmaker. To make matters worse, his knee was hurt. That Italian team stumbled its way into the cup and quickly stumbled its way out.

It should come as no surprise—we being Argentines and they being Italians—that there was a lot of talk on the field during that game. Plus, we knew each other well. Bagni and Ruggeri had a few nice run-ins. Bagni told me to tell El Cabezón that he was a *figlio di puttana*, as if Ruggeri wouldn't be able to figure that out, and El Cabezón asked me what he could call him to get him riled up. "No, Cabezón, don't call him anything… Or maybe just *cornuto*." Every time Salvatore would come close, Ruggeri would say to me, "Aaahhh, look, the *cornuto* is coming over to mark me." Drove him crazy.

A bunch of guys from Juve—like Scirea and Cabrini—played for the Italian team, as did some players for Inter—Bergomi and Altobelli. De Napoli, who would later come to Napoli to play with me, was also playing in the South, for Avellino. From Verona, which was a popular team at the time, came Di Gennaro and Galderisi, and Galli was the goalie for Fiorentina; Bruno Conti—a great guy, I give him a big hug whenever I see him—was the star at Roma. Before the World Cup, when everyone was talking about who might really stand out, I couldn't believe that they didn't mention him. He was an innovative player for that time, with a style that was hard to pin down. And he had been on the championship team in '82, at the cup where Gentile had hacked the shit out of me. And that also weighed on me.

But Gentile wasn't typical. Most of the Italian defenders tried to take the ball from you with class; they were master markers, it was like an art form for them. Cabrini, the *fidanzato* of Italy—they called him "the boyfriend of Italy" in those days—was a sophisticated but ruthless player.

And there was Vierchowod—my God, Vierchowod! He was great at recovering the ball, and had huge, tremendous legs. He was the son of a Ukrainian who had fought for the Red Army, but was Italian by birth. A Soviet-style bulldog turned solid as a rock, Italian-style. He was great at recovering the ball and he would then pass it on to a teammate, always without a hitch. He was a hard worker and a first-rate marker.

I talked a lot about him, before the game, with "El Bichi" Borghi. I mean a lot. Because at that point in the cup—and it's good to go over this so the truth comes out about how the team was put together—journalists and everyone else were putting lots of pressure on Bilardo to have Borghi play with me. And I wanted to play with him. I really pampered him, because he needed it—he needed a lot of attention. He was still just a kid and Bilardo didn't know how to handle him. I remember I even lent him something Dal Monte had made to stabilize my ankle—Borghi's ankles were giving way all the time.

The thing is that Bilardo put him in as a starter against Italy. With Valdano upfield. The rest of the lineup was Nery as goalie, Cuciuffo in for Clausen, Brown and Ruggeri—who were untouchable—and Garré. Giusti, Batista, Burruchaga, and Maradona, by heart. And Jorge Valdano with Borghi.

So I went up to El Bichi and said, "Vierchowod is going to mark you. It's easy to get past him with the ball, especially with your skill. But it's easy for him to catch back up with you—got it?"

"Got it," he said.

"Listen, you hook the ball and get past him, but if you hook it again, he goes ping and when you look up, he's right in front of you again—got it?"

"Got it."

"I'm telling you this because he marked me and the first three times I got possession that same thing happened . . . The fourth time, I did the old one-two, and ran off with the ball."

I don't know if he got what I was saying, but I do know that his moves kept Vierchowod busy. "El Bichi" Borghi was extremely talented, but he was sort of distracted that game, and the next one too.

What did happen in that game against Italy, though, was that we started to believe in ourselves. It was the second game in the cup, after beating the Koreans good. We were strong against a team that may not have been at its peak but did have plenty of experience and knew how to play the game.

We were solid on defense, active at midfield, and aggressive upfield. Clausen was not one of the starting defenders, after playing a very weak first game. I loved Clausen, but in Mexico he didn't start off like the tank he was playing fullback for Independiente. Cuciuffo came in and started to earn himself a spot on the team; he didn't play as a stopper yet, but he did take care of Galderisi. We stuck with four men on defense, with "El Tata" Brown freer and "El Cabezón" Ruggeri—who ate Altobelli alive—as centers and Garré on the left wing, against Bruno Conti.

Each of us played where he felt he had to. Burruchaga played more to the left, and that was very important to our offense, more so than against the Koreans. "El Checho" Batista seemed a bit uncomfortable, and Bilardo took him out at the beginning of the second half. Batista was so pissed, he even threatened to go back to Buenos Aires. That's the way the group was: everyone was a leader; we were always setting limits on what Bilardo could and could not do.

The idea was that Borghi and I would have possession of the ball and attack quickly, which Valdano couldn't do: he didn't have our sprinting skills but he did take big steps that could make a real difference upfield. They wanted El Bichi to start farther back and, in the end, he didn't know where he was playing.

That's why, for all the talk about Bilardo's savvy tactics, I don't see it that way.

Valdano himself explained it really well in an interview he did with *La Nación* twenty years after the cup. It might take me another twenty to explain it, but he put it just right— like a philosopher—so I'll just quote it: "How a group of scattered individuals could come together as an inviolable team," is what he said. I couldn't agree more with his description. He used complicated words, but his message is clear as day.

We players were the ones who won that World Cup, and it was at that game that we started to realize what we were capable of, and to make others realize it too. Some players were starting to play better than at the pre-cup tour. But it was at that game against the world champions—which Italy still was at that point—that we showed them what we were made of.

We were able to get over the penalty kick for a foul that Dutch son of a bitch Jan Keizer made up. My buddy Conti was trying to get the ball from Garré at the edge of the penalty area. He managed to block it, but the ball bounced off onto Burruchaga's hand. Burru didn't try to touch the ball—the ball hit him, but the guy called the foul. I think the power wielded by the Italian team played a role there. Back then, the refs were soft on Italy and on Brazil. Do you know where the Italian team was staying? In Puebla. Do you know what hotel they were staying at? The Mesón del Ángel. Do you know where Keizer stayed when he went to Puebla? That's right, at the Mesón del Ángel.

THAT'S HOW WE STARTED TO WIN THE CUP

Six minutes in, nothing doing, and Altobelli scores. Altobelli, of all people—one of my long-standing rivals during my Italian club days and now a regular guest at my home in Dubai. He is a commentator on Italian soccer for belN Sports, and I love watching the games, especially when Italian clubs are playing. Every time I see him on the screen, I remember that time it could have all gone to shit on the field in Puebla—but that's not how it went. And it wasn't by chance: we knew what was going on and we were able to keep things under control.

"We're going to keep possession of the ball, nice and easy. No need to lose your head," I told Burruchaga.

You always have to respect Italy, even when it's not in its heyday. Or, rather, not respect it. Go right over it. The Italians are like the Germans: as soon as they smell victory, they get cocky. And they made us bleed with that goal right at the beginning. I mean, in just one minute it could all come back to haunt us. It didn't really mean much that we had beaten South Korea; we were still, basically, a team that few had faith in—just us, in fact.

That's why that game mattered so much. A one to one tie was like a win because of how we played, because of how we bounced back from that first goal. My goal, which tied it up, wasn't until after the half-hour mark. The ball began with "El Gringo" Giusti, from there it went to Borghi, and ended in a pass—no booter, in my opinion—that Valdano sent my way. I've already described the goal. I've already said that it was one of the sweetest and most important of my career.

That was also when we began winning the World Cup. We could win the game. No way we were playing defensively. If someone on the bench had motioned for us to lay back, I would have been burned up. We were burning up the field and were close to scoring a few times. Valdano headed a ball that came pretty close, and Ruggeri and Brown were right on every set piece.

When the game was almost over, Vialli went over to Garré and said to him *"Pareggio,* Garré, *pareggio. Parla con* Bilardo."

"Pareggio, my ass. We're going to win it," Garré replied. If he had said anything to Bilardo, I would have killed him. I swear I would have. Because that's what I wanted—a mighty team, a team that would break its opponents' balls.

Bilardo took Batista out of this game as well. And Batista went nuts, because he thought it was another one of Bilardo's infamous superstitions. That was when Batista said he wanted to go home. They had a meeting and Bilardo, jerk that he was, asked me to be there, because he always wanted a witness. He was paranoid.

But when I watch the game now—for the first time, I actually sat down and watched it—I am as pleased as I was back then. With that tie we sent a message, to ourselves but mostly to the other teams, to our rivals: "If we tied the Italians, and we could well have beaten them, we can rival the big teams, the contenders."

There had been a lot of talk about the fact that the Mexicans didn't root for us. And that's true, but only partly. Against South Korea, it made sense since people always root for the underdog, especially when there's a big difference. The same thing when we played against Bulgaria. But in the game against Italy—when we were the upstarts and we played at the same level—they started out rooting for them but ended up rooting for us. They realized that we were the ones giving it our all for the game; we were the ones setting the pace.

Beyond all that, Ruggeri was, in my view, the star of that game. He had played great against the Koreans, scoring a goal and all, and in this game he had to take care of Altobelli, who only managed to score one goal with a penalty kick. Other than that, he barely touched the ball. What's more, he ended up having to mark "El Cabezón" Ruggeri, who was going upfield every chance he got, to try to score again. He wanted to score goals, the madman! He had blind faith in himself and he managed to get his way all the time. He was in rare form.

By this time, I was really quick out there, thanks to all the training I had done in preparation for the cup. In the lead-up to the cup, they had changed how I trained, what I ate, how I hydrated. What I did to prepare for the cup was unheard of in Argentina—it had never been done before and there was no way to do it in the country. It was not common for a player to go to such lengths.

In soccer today, I see a lot of physical training but not much technique. In my day, it was different: the emphasis was on technique, which is why you could make a real difference if you were in great shape. It is also why Pep Guardiola stands out so much today and inspires such admiration. Soccer today is rushed, not quick—and it's not the same thing. They rush down to goal, and that's not the way the game should be played. What matters is getting to the rival's goal in good form, not fast.

But in '86 I was in good form and fast and—believe it or not—in '90 I was even better. But the problems I had with my toenail and with my ankle affected me. To say nothing of everything else I had to deal with. I was, by that time, the devil, *il diavolo*, as that cover of *La Gazzetta dello Sport* put it.

Salvatore Carmando, my masseuse from Naples, went through the same thing as me. In Naples, they didn't like him from the get-go, which is why he came with me. In '86, they didn't give him the time of day, but in '90 they took him with them—they remembered he was Italian.

I WAS THE EMBLEM OF THE SOUTH

For the powerful North, what we did with Napoli was a real blow. It hurt. And they didn't just love me in Naples; they loved me from there on down. All of poor southern Italy loved me. I was their emblem. The emblem of the poor South against the powerful North, the one who took from the rich

North to give to the poor South. They still love me—that was for keeps.

Until '86, Juve would visit San Paolo stadium, score three goals, and head back home; then they would go to Milan, score, and head home; same with Inter. When I got there and the team came together the way it did, things turned around and they started coming after me. We'd score three or four goals against them at a single game. Juve, Milan, Inter—whoever. In the final at the Supercoppa, we scored five against Juve. That was historic.

Starting then, right when we began winning, they wanted to kill me. In '90 more than ever. And in '91, Matarrese and Ferlaino made me pay. It was a really terrible organization. They didn't pay me a single lira when I left Italy and I had to leave everything behind. I didn't ask for anything either. I just left, not a word.

Then they made Cani pay as well—Caniggia. It's messed up. Only two players of a total of ten thousand tested positive.

Come on! The whole thing was probably payback for all the lucrative deals they lost because of us in '90. Even a blind man would be able to see that.

Even today, Italians—whether from the South or from the North—always treat me with great respect, regardless of everything they put me through. I am not, for them, a soccer player but a legend. In that sense, the Italians are very respectful. It really touches my heart that they still look at me as if I could do today what I did on the field back then. That really warms my heart. I have experienced that in Italy and in England too. It's strange, different. But it's nice to be recognized like that.

In 2011, my daughter Dalma insisted on going to Naples; she wanted to go back to that city she had left at the age of two. And I said to her, "No, baby cakes, better go somewhere else. The people in Naples are really expressive and they're going to drive you crazy. Visit other cities." But, like her father Maradona, she wouldn't be talked out of it. "No, Dad, Naples goes nuts when you visit, but who knows me there? We left when I was two and nobody will realize who I am. Don't worry, I'll stay with friends and nobody will even know I was there. I want to visit it all; I can't remember a thing about Naples."

And, you know what? I was right! Dalma had to admit it. If in Argentina I get plenty of unconditional love, all the more so in Naples. When they found out she was in town, she couldn't walk down the street. People would kneel down before her. Dalma would help them up and tell them to calm down. After all, what had she done?

The first day, they took her sightseeing and stopped the car in front of a building. "Let's get out here," they said. They got in the elevator and rang a doorbell on the second floor; when the door opened, all the neighbors on that floor were there, waiting for her with hugs and kisses, photos, then more hugs and kisses, and more photos . . .

Dalma was gracious, assuming that they had known her when she was little. They had photos of us, of the family, of the girls, in their homes. When she had said hello to everyone, she got in the elevator to leave, relieved that it was over, but no. They went up to the third floor, and the same thing all over again: hugs and kisses, photos, more hugs and kisses, more photos. And so on, one floor at a time, up to the seventh floor—the most "intense" of all the floors. There was a display case with photos of us—it even had grass I had stepped on in it! She said good-bye and was sure it was over and that she could do some sightseeing. But no. They took her to a hospital. And when they got there, everyone was waiting at the door: doctors, technicians, nurses, and even patients. And no one would settle for a group shot—each wanted their own little picture!

It was a Tuesday and they opened the stadium just for her. She told them that she was the daughter of a soccer player who had played there, but at first they didn't believe her. If it had been Gianinna, my other daughter, she would have said, "You know what? My name is Maradona—let me in!" But Dalma just showed them her passport. The guy almost dropped dead on the spot. She was startled when she saw a sort of "shrine" at the stadium, with photos of the years I played for the team.

Before heading home, they went to get something to eat at a shopping mall, and people started bringing her gifts—soccer jerseys and trophies. They even gave her a thumb drive with photos of their entire families for me to see, one by one. When Dalma had thanked each and every one of the people who had brought her gifts, she realized that it wouldn't be possible to take all the stuff with her, because she was in the middle of her trip. "Ma non preoccuparti," they told her, and they gave her a suitcase where she could put everything. That's what Neapolitans are like.

She was so surprised by what she experienced on that trip that she got the idea for the play *Hija de Dios* (Daughter of God), where she told it all. The title got her into trouble with some knuckleheads—you can imagine. "Does she really think she's the daughter of God?" And the whole play is about how, for her, her dad is just her dad, nothing else, not God. I cried from the moment I stepped foot in the theater until I left.

The worst thing about the trip was not that she never got a chance to see Naples the way she wanted to, since the people barely let her walk down the street. The worst thing was that she had to admit Dad was right! And, stubborn as she is, she didn't want to admit I was right when I asked her, "Baby, how did it go in Naples?" She just said, "Nice, very nice."

DO AT FIFA WHAT FRANCISCO IS DOING AT THE VATICAN

Plenty of other things have changed over the years. When I talk about Italy, I talk about Rome. And if I talk about Rome, I talk about the Vatican. Everyone knows what I thought about the Vatican in '86. I wouldn't even have a coffee with that pope—the one I visited and shook hands with back then—even if they gave me my weight in gold. But now that Francisco's pope, the coffee's on me.

The pope we have today asks himself why we need a Vatican Bank. At least he asks the question. And he got rid of a guy who was spending eight thousand euros a month. I mean, Maradona might take home eighty thousand euros a month, but a priest, who doesn't have to support a home or put food on the table, who has all of his expenses covered, what does he want money for, if not to help the poor?

I loved that. I love it that this pope takes care of the things he should take care of, of the needy.

The guy, Francisquito, as I like to call him—with all the respect in the world—is doing things the way they should be done. They brought him some red shoes from Prada or something, and he said he already had shoes, a pair of moccasins that he had bought in Boedo, in Buenos Aires, that he found perfectly comfortable. That's great.

One night, he got past his guards and people saw a little old priest eating a slice of pizza on the street. Another day he went to an ordinary, everyday optician's shop to get a pair of glasses made.

I identify with all that, but it also scares me because death can be hiding around any corner for good popes. And I told Francisquito as much. He told me not to worry, that he knew how to take care of himself and that he was keeping everyone in line.

I felt the whole time that he was speaking from the heart—and that's what matters most.

The pope is doing at the Vatican what I would like to do at FIFA. Bring transparency. So that the people are the winners. In the case of FIFA, that means no more bribes or fixed World Cup matches. Just as the pope helps the starving around the world, the leaders of the soccer industry should take care of the guys playing and the people watching them play. If they want an entertaining World Cup, that's great, but it has to be won fair and square—not bought. If it's about the money, the cup would always be played in the United Arab Emirates because nobody's got more dough than them.

When I went to visit Francisco and I walked into the Vatican, I didn't see the gold ceilings. Because he welcomed me with a handshake in a little room where anyone—the two most ordinary guys in the world—might meet. We talked about everything. He told me that he needed me and that Argentina needed us both. He told me that two Argentines had

© Revista El Gráfico

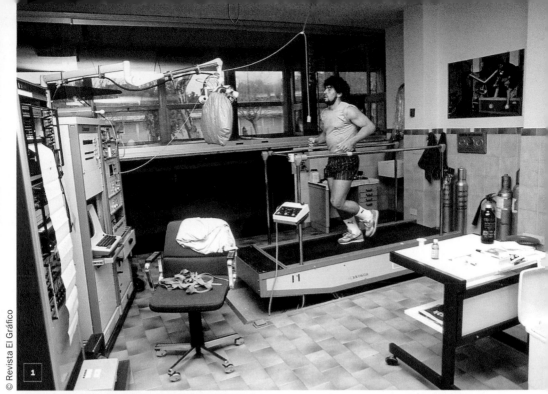

© Revista El Gráfico

© Revista El Gráfico

1   There were three months to go before the World Cup when I started training with Professor Dal Monte. Every Monday, I would travel to his clinic in Rome. I had a very specific training routine, and the Argentine national team was my top priority. That's why when I got to Mexico, I was in amazing shape ... I could fly down the field!

2   Our last exhibition game was in Barranquilla, and it ended in a tie. But we won a much more important battle that day: we players got together after the match and decided we had to get back to the training camp. At that meeting, the champion team was born.

3   At Club América, Bilardo wouldn't let us train. One day, I went into the equipment room and asked for a ball. The guys didn't want to give it to me because they were afraid of what the coach would say. I took the ball anyway and put together a pickup game. We would later run our victory lap around those same fields—all by ourselves.

© Revista El Gráfico

© Revista El Gráfico

4 When *El Gráfico* wanted to do the now-famous photo with the Mexican sombreros for the magazine cover, I started to feel like I was really the captain and Passarella was long gone. That's why I didn't mind being in a picture with him. I chose the mustard-colored sombrero, because it had one of Boca's colors. Passarella doesn't grin much in the photo because his teeth were crooked—or so he said.

5 After the photo shoot, Passarella left. He didn't want to talk to the reporters because he said we had to practice. Ha. We had time to talk but he didn't want to stick around.

6 Passarella didn't practice as much as me. Then he started talking about Montezuma's revenge and who knows what. And right before our first game against South Korea, he pulled a muscle. Come on! Thank goodness "El Tata" Brown was there. No one believed in him but me.

7 Take a look at this one, the complete lineup. Not all of our uniforms matched. There were a lot of kids on that team: not a lot of aces, but everyone had something to say. There was always some excuse for a meeting.

8 My old man, the best guy in the world. He was the only one from my family I let come to the World Cup because I needed to concentrate on my game. And he was also the only one who said—even before the Cup started—that our biggest rival would be West Germany. You can't imagine how that came back to me before the final game!

9 Now everyone talks about players' diets ... I didn't worry much about my diet: I liked the pastas that Carmando, my masseuse, would make, and the meats that my old man would grill. It was a ritual: we would eat right next to the training fields.

© Revista El Gráfico

© Revista El Gráfico

© Revista El Gráfico

© Revista El Gráfico

© Revista El Gráfico

© AFP

© Revista El Gráfico

10 There were no cell phones back then! And there was only one phone at the whole training camp: we would wait in line to make a call. And boy, the shit really hit the fan with Passarella's calls to Italy. Here I am on the phone while "El Vasco" Olarticoechea—one of our star players—waits his turn.

11 The equipment room was one of my favorite spots at the training camp. The rest of the boys and I would go in there to drink mate with Tito Benrós and Nery.

12 We'd go to the mall the day before each game and get an ice cream at Helen's—it brought us good luck.

13 Going to eat at Cremasco's restaurant after each game was another ritual. And Galíndez would put together his show.

14 This is my favorite photo—I've got it, poster sized, hanging in my room. Valdano used to say that when I did tricks with the ball, it was like I was making love to it. And there's something to that … When I was playing, even at the World Cup, I felt like a little boy.

15 At the beginning, hardly any reporters came to talk to us, but once we started winning, they started coming. A press room? No way! One day I made them stand on the other side of the fence and answered their questions there. I was wearing the Italian jersey, after swapping with Bagni. Imagine that happening now.

© Getty Images

16 Boy, those South Koreans really lit into me! I get sore all over again just watching the game. And I even wore bandages up over my socks ... but they kicked me in unthinkable places. This kick came about three minutes into the match. It took me a while to get up after that one, and then the goal was scored. It was essential to win that first game against South Korea. Imagine what the media would have said about us if we had lost to the South Koreans! They would have butchered us. We had to start winning right from the get-go. "El Cabezón" Ruggeri scored an awesome goal and started showing what he would be capable of during the entire World Cup.

© Revista El Gráfico

© Corbis

17 and 18 Goalie Giovanni Galli looks like he's made of stone here but there was nothing he could have done. It was all Scirea's fault. Thanks to the curl I put on the ball, I score five out of every ten shots on goal. Only five, just half. What I mean is that if I do it again, if I kick the ball in the exact same way, half the time I will be standing there cursing because I missed it and half the time I will be screaming my head off, ecstatic about the goal I just scored. I'm really talking about the goal I scored against Italy, one of the best goals of my life. And one of the goals I celebrated the most as well.

© Revista El Gráfico

© Revista El Gráfico

19 The time has come to tell our experience on the ground and not just Bilardo's vision. I want to make this clear here and now: I did not stab Bilardo in the back when the government called me about getting rid of him. He, on the other hand, left me feeling betrayed almost thirty years later.

20 Beating the Bulgarians was just a formality, and the game was a real bore. But we qualified without having lost a single game. There's nothing greater than heading off to the locker room like that, with your hands curled into fists. And with the backing of "El Profe" Echevarría—an amazing guy and a key member of the coaching staff.

21 Sometimes putting a curl on the ball and positioning your body just right makes all the difference. In the game against Uruguay, I made my way upfield on the right wing and passed to the center with my left foot to get around the defender who was closing in and the goalie who had come out of the box. Pedrito Pasculli missed his chance for another goal. That was my best game in the World Cup—we should have won by a much larger margin.

© Revista El Gráfico

22 There's a picture I always remember, a really great, special shot: the two teams are walking into the stadium, up some sort of ramp installed behind an arch. There were 115,000 people in the stands, but all I could hear was the clicking of our cleats on that metallic floor. There was no more talking at that point, not between us players or to any of them.

© Revista El Gráfico

23

© Revista El Gráfico

24

23 I had never seen this photo of the goal against the English before. It's right when I hook past Shilton instead of kicking. Shilton made things easy for me because he just stood there like a bump on a log ... And then Butcher came in for the kill. I didn't even realize how hard he had hit my ankle until I got back to the locker room.

24 When I ran off to celebrate, right near the corner I bumped into Salvatore Carmando, who was there watching the game. He kissed me on the forehead. Now that's one great *Napolitano* ...

25 I went to take a corner kick against the English, but the corner flag was in my way so I pulled it up and threw it on the ground. Ulloa, the assistant referee, came over to make me put the flag back in its place. "Okay, I'll put it back. And at the next World Cup, I'll be playing as a linesman."

© Revista El Gráfico
© Revista El Gráfico
© Revista El Gráfico

26 Guys like Messi, Tevez, and Riquelme can come in here now and score ten goals each. Better goals than that one. But we were playing against the English, after a war—after a war that was still fresh in everyone's mind, a war in which seventeen-year-old boys had gone out to fight in Flecha tennis shoes, shooting pellets at the English, who decided how many Argentine boys they would kill and how many they would let live—and there's nothing that can compare to that. Parents told their children about it, and those children will tell their children. Because thirty years have already gone by. Thirty years. And they keep on telling the story.

27 When the game against the English ended, I started celebrating like a madman. For me, it was as if we had won the final. And on the way to the sidelines, I ran into "El Ciego" Signorini, my trainer. I was in unbelievable shape. At that point in the World Cup, I truly felt like no one could stop me.

© Getty Images

© Revista El Gráfico

28 In the first goal against Belgium, I ran in on a diagonal, and as soon as two of their defenders closed in (now I see that it was Veyt and Demol) and Pfaff came running out in a craze, I smacked the ball sideways, with my left foot, high up. The secret to that goal was beating the two defenders to the ball. I saw Pfaff coming over to block me and I chipped it past him.

29 We were there to play the final under that giant spider that everyone probably remembers because it cast a shadow over us. As soon as the anthem was finished, El Tata and I started yelling. We crouched down and leaned forward, and shouted, "Let's go get 'em, man. Let's do it!" We were like eleven madmen ready for war.

30 Check out the penalty play—the penalty shot Arppi Filho didn't call because he's a cock-sucker. I was running circles around them. Valdano, Burruchaga, and I put together a great play: I went right past the Germans; one of them fouled me, but I recovered the ball and headed straight for Schumacher. Right then, Jakobs was moving in as well. I tapped the ball and Schumacher plowed right into me. Man, that was a penalty, hands-down.

31 I said it then and I'll say it again now, thirty years later: that was the peak of my career. Because of the way we won it too ... How could I not have cried?

© Revista El Gráfico

32 "This one is for you / all you / motherfuckers." That chant was like our national anthem, especially on the trip home. All us troublemakers were in the back at first, but we soon took over the entire plane, even the first-class cabin where all the suits were. It was quite the group. Just the way I wanted it.

33 and 34 I flew home with the cup in my arms, cradling it like a baby. I didn't want to give it to anyone. We got on the plane the very night we won the cup. All we cared about was getting back to Argentina and celebrating with all the people who had rooted for us. I got off the plane at Ezeiza airport, cup in hand; the number of fans was mind-boggling. It was sure different from the send-off they had given us ...

35 Whenever I was afraid, I would think of my Mom, Tota. "Come on, Tota, help me," I would say to myself. But I knew she wasn't there because I had asked her to stay in Buenos Aires. She was the first one I embraced when I got to Ezeiza airport. When I saw her waiting there, I burst into tears.

© Pablo Grinberg

36

36 When I walked out onto the balcony of the Casa Rosada, the president's office, cup in hand, I felt like Juan Domingo Perón when he would go out there to talk to the masses. I've been a Peronist my whole life and I'll die a Peronist, because of my mother and because of Evita. In our sexist society, everyone talks about Perón, but Evita was a great woman.

© Getty Images

37 I may have been polished at the World Cup, at the top of my game, but it was because I had trained to get there. If I had to give Messi some advice on how to win in Russia, which he very well could do, I'd tell him to take a few months off beforehand to train with the national team. What could they possibly say about that in Barcelona, when he's given them his all? It doesn't please me in the slightest that Argentina hasn't brought the cup home in thirty years. If it did, I'd be a traitor. I would love for there to be one more star above the crest on our jersey.

never been at the top level internationally at the same time, the way he and I were then.

The truth is, I want the pope to be more famous than Maradona. But I have an edge, which is that I played soccer pretty well. And soccer is a worldwide passion.

CHAPTER 5

Playing against FIFA

ARGENTINA 2, BULGARIA 0
—Mexico City, Tuesday, June 10

It was in Mexico that I started making trouble for FIFA. We had played against South Korea and they had hacked us to a pulp. So I complained about the violence. Then we played against Italy and the referee was awful, which was why I made a scene with the heavy hitters in soccer in Europe and Brazil. Then came the game against Bulgaria, at Olímpico stadium again, just like our first game. They made us play at midday—at midday, at that altitude and with all that smog! Those bastards! I mean, something really bad could have happened, no joke.

WE WERE BEAT; THEY WERE EATING CAVIAR AND DRINKING CHAMPAGNE

I remember that we got to talking in the training camp. That was where the uprising began, where we began to realize that we had amazing power. If we said "we won't play anymore," everything would have come to an end. I mean everything.

That was what "El Ciego" Signorini said when he came by the room to talk to Pedrito Pasculli, Valdano, and me.

Valdano wasn't one to say what he really thought. And, truth be told, I wanted to be like him. But my legs were my weapons and my bullet the ball. If we called it quits, it wouldn't do much good because people wanted to see us play. What was the best approach? We had to play but we also had to speak out, never shut up. So I confronted João Havelange for the first time. About the violence, about the referees, and about the schedule.

"Players are here to play—that's it. We're the ones who make the rules, the ones to do the talking," he said, asshole that he was.

He should never have said that!

"Listen, don Havelange, we players are nobody's slaves, especially not yours," I replied. "The least you can do is listen to what we have to say. If we're wrong, we'll keep quiet, end of story."

Like hell I was going to keep quiet, of course, but that was how I had to play it. To make things perfectly clear, I also said that he couldn't be a dictator—it took guts to call that guy a dictator back then. He was in charge of everything and the most powerful guy at FIFA. If he wanted to take you down, you went down. He was badder than the baddest defenders we would come up against.

If they changed the time of a game so that people in China could watch it on TV, that was fine with us, because we also wanted them to see us. But they could have moved it back a few hours or something so we didn't have to play at twelve noon. I mean, playing at noon with the altitude and the smog was downright criminal. We were beat by the end. During

the last twenty minutes of play, some of the guys were re-
duced to walking; it was scary to see the vacant stares in
their eyes. And the FIFA officials were sitting in their boxes,
air-conditioning blasting, drinking champagne and eating
caviar. Until I, a poor kid from Villa Fiorito, came up to them
to say, "That's fine, eat your expensive caviar and drink the
best bubbly, but we want to put on a good show for the people
without killing ourselves trying."

And putting on a good show under the noonday sun in the
heat was no mean feat.

Back then, even Julio Grondona admitted that I was
right. At least he didn't tell me to shut up. But, come to think
of it, he might have been playing it both ways, telling me I
was right when we were alone together and telling the FIFA
officials that they were right when he was with them. That
wouldn't surprise me. Besides, he knew, because I had told
him, that we would do our best on the field regardless. We
would play to win, because if we won, they would listen to us.
If we didn't, they might think we were crybabies. And one
thing I have never been is a crybaby. We were rebels, but we
knew that we also had to be professional and responsible.

JUST LIKE THE CEBOLLITAS, BUT ADULT SIZE

One thing that did make me cry, though, was getting up early
in the morning. And to play at noon meant getting up at seven
in the morning—no way around it. At seven fifteen, Trobbiani and Valdano, who were early risers, would be at the door
to the room. I loved shaving outside—something I picked up
from my dad on the days he would go fishing. At the training
camp, there was no choice because not every room had a

bathroom. So that was the first ritual on game days. Then a shower and breakfast. More like lunch than breakfast, since we had to be able to play four hours later. I would often ask Carmando to make me some pasta, real Italian-style, and I would down it at that hour—which is why I say to hell with special diets! There was something—how should I put it?—amateur about the whole thing. It was like we were the Cebollitas, but adult size. We were having fun even though we complained about everything.

Same thing with the uniforms. If you see the team photo today, the official lineup before starting the cup, you wouldn't believe it. Bilardo and some of the coaching staff were wearing different brands from us. That Argentine team—the one that is engraved in the memory of all Argentines—got as far as it did with almost no clothes! That's how it was for us.

By that time, we were so tight as a group that nothing could pull us apart—nothing from within our ranks or outside them. Once I got over my early morning bad mood, the bus trip to the stadium was sheer happiness. They used to say—and still do—that Islas was resentful and would complain, just like the other guys who didn't see any play—guys like Almirón and Zelada. But, in fact, they were the most enthusiastic, the guys who cheered the loudest. We had put together a really solid group.

That Tuesday, June 10, after shaving outside, showering, and having Carmando's pasta for breakfast, Pasculli and I embraced, as always, before the bus took off for the stadium. As I said, it wasn't far away, which was great. And the ride there was part of the celebration. We were feeling pretty self-confident by this point, and we all looked at each other with respect. The game against Italy had gone well, and Bilardo didn't change the lineup: Nery as goalie; Cuciuffo and Garré as fullbacks; Brown and Ruggeri as center backs; "El Gringo" Giusti, "Checho" Batista, and Burruchaga at midfield; me, covering the whole field; and Borghi and Valdano playing forward.

The Bulgarians looked scared of us, especially in the players' tunnel, on the way out to the field, when "El Tata" Brown and I started fooling around and a bunch of the others joined in. What did I do? I jumped on his back and started shouting like a gorilla; then I climbed off and started beating my chest. Next thing we knew, we were all screaming like madmen. "Let's go get 'em!!! Let's go to it!!!" The Bulgarians looked terrified.

It started out as a joke, but we ended up taking it seriously. I recently found out that the guys from Argentina's Olympic basketball team, Generación Dorada—who are amazing—used to do something similar.

When the referee—Berny Ulloa from Costa Rica—gave the word for us to come out, I remember I said to Brown, "It's all good, Tata. We're going to win this thing."

"Don't get cocky, Diego. You always tell us not to let our guard down."

"Yeah, I know, but I'm not saying it because of us. I'm saying it because of them. Take a look at these guys."

The truth is, we didn't know much about the Bulgarian team. We knew Georgi Yordanov—we had him pegged—but nobody else, really.

As predicted, we took control of the game against Bulgaria quickly, with a goal by Valdano right away. But if you watch the game again, as I did, you'll see that we were still running after the ball like a bunch of savages. I don't want to say anything against Bilardo, because everyone's going to say, "There goes Maradona, thinking he won the cup on his own." But that's not true. We all won the world championship together, as a team. I was the cherry on top, and nobody can take that away from me. But that's a long cry from saying we were a well-oiled machine thanks to Bilardo's training sessions during the week. Come on! He wouldn't even let us train!

Anyway, we were beating the poor, frightened Bulgarians, one to nothing, three minutes in. In those few minutes, Cuciuffo rushed one of their fullbacks and stole the ball from him. He looked up and kicked center Garrincha-style, and Valdano headed the ball in. It was incredible. I see it now and it's like a frozen frame, like a photo. He jumped as high as the crossbar, like Michael Jordan or something.

And Cuciuffo turned out to be a monster player, another of the cup's surprises. He hadn't expected to play much, but he ended up marking like Beckenbauer and kicking to center like Zico.

That game against Bulgaria was not so spectacular, actually. It allowed us to qualify for the next round—that's it. But we didn't play any better than we had against Italy. It was partly the Bulgarians' fault, since they were satisfied with losing by a little. It was partly the fault of the weather, which was hot and humid. The best part was that play by Cuciuffo and another thing, the defensive line, the center backs. Brown and Ruggeri nailed it. Also, I found an ally in Valdano. Jorge was able to make contact, not only with the ball, but also with me. And he headed in that amazing shot.

The guy who didn't shine in the cup was "El Bichi" Borghi. He only played in the first period; then Bilardo took him out. And he didn't put him back in. Too bad, because

Borghi was extremely talented. Maybe that cup came before his prime. Bilardo also took out "Checho" Batista. I mean, he was always taking him out, and Checho didn't like that one bit. I didn't either, though I began to understand that it was important to make a place for "El Vasco" Olarticoechea, who would come in for Batista, and Enrique, who would come in for Borghi. But I don't know—or, actually, I do—if the changes were about the players per se. But we would find our way later on.

The thing was to qualify and come out on top in our group. I didn't like tight games. Luckily, half an hour into the second period, when we were all taking a nap, I took off from the left— which I used to love to do—almost like an outside forward or a left winger, as they're called these days. We had recovered the ball at midfield and Valdano back-heeled it to Garré, and he booted it. I bolted to the ball, kicked it past number 6 on one side, and then caught up with it on the other side, heading deep, but not before looking up to see who was coming. I passed center. Burruchaga was the guy who made it there first, to head it in, just as Valdano had done. And that was another good sign, because Burru hadn't had many chances at a goal. When he played for Independiente, he was upfield like a for- ward, but he was having trouble letting it rip for the national team. But he was worth waiting for. In my view, nobody else on the team played like him, with that combination of skills. He just had to start playing, really playing, in the World Cup—and that, if you ask me, was when the cup started.

We had come out on top in our group, but it was in the quarterfinals that it got real heavy. Unlike four years earlier, in Spain in '82, when we came up against Brazil and Italy in the quarterfinals, this time it was do or die.

This is why I called another meeting, another serious meeting. And I got right to the point:

"Fellows, things go our way when we play the way we want to—isn't that right? So if Bilardo tells us to lay back and stick to defense, we're going to head upfield and attack. If not, who the hell are we, Burkina Faso? We're going to play to win, man. Because now it's do or die. If we don't win now, everything we've done so far isn't worth shit."

Even Passarella agreed with me, not to mention Bochini. "El Tata" Brown defended Bilardo—and looking back I can see why, and I am sure he now understands my point of view too. I had Brown's back as much as Bilardo did. It was because of the faith I had in him, in "El Cabezón" Ruggeri, in "Cuchu" Cuciuffo, that I knew we could go for it and take a few more risks out there.

I was all in, on the field and off it.

BIG BUCKS FOR THE FAMILY (THE FIFA FAMILY)

Getting back to the FIFA issue, and looking back at everything that has happened over the course of these thirty years, I think what's been missing is player unity, players rallying together the way we did in Mexico. They have tried to buy me off a number of times over the years. Even at the cerebration of the hundredth anniversary of AFA, where they gave me a medal—I thanked them and made nice because it had to do with the history of soccer, not politics!—they tried to buy me off. It was '93 and the national team was playing against Denmark in Mar del Plata, and then against Brazil at Monumental stadium. They gave me a medal for being the best player in history, and then they locked me up in a room with Havelange.

Sepp Blatter was there too. And they told me, "Dieguito, we want you to be part of the FIFA family."

"Thanks, guys, but I've already got a family."

"But, listen, Dieguito, the guys who form part of the FIFA family make big bucks."

"Listen, thanks for the offer, but you must be confused. You see, I play soccer for a living. I earn money kicking a ball around. And I kick it pretty good."

Grondona was waiting for me when I came out.

"What happened, Diego?" he asked.

"Nothing at all, Julio. Nothing at all."

And nothing did happen, until now. That's why I say a lot of players should have been as clear as I was that time. And a good number were, actually. And there are a lot of good guys, like Didier Drogba, who is phenomenal. He took his struggle way beyond soccer. I mean, if you see what that guy did for the Ivory Coast, you have to take your hat off to him. Now that's using soccer for a good cause, not the way politicians use it. He used soccer to bring people together in a country where they were gunning each other down. Romário too. He got involved in politics and used it to defend the sport before the World Cup in Brazil, for example, sending all the corrupt officials, the guys who filled their pockets—or wanted to—from the sport, to jail. And I can't leave out Hristo Stoichkov, who—like me—has always been a rebel, a fighter.

But check this out: the guy who swapped his shorts for a suit and tie was Platini, the lowest of the low. Even thirty years ago, I could tell he had no guts, what with his perfumes and his finesse. The thing is, Platini always wanted to play it both ways, eating caviar and drinking champagne but also wanting to be seen with us, the players, who stood our ground and would go out on strike if necessary. He played both sides. Or he wanted to.

That's why I really wanted to beat Platini on the field, to show him there in Mexico who the better player was. We were true rivals, because we both wore the number 10 and because we couldn't have been more different when we took our jerseys off. In terms of play, my rivals were Zico, Rummenigge, and maybe Laudrup—but he was still a kid. The thing is, Zico was a great guy, who would invite you over and goof off, introduce you to his kids. Platini's another story. I have never met his kids, his wife, or looked at his bank accounts.

That's why I would have liked to be part of a different FIFA. But not part of "the FIFA family," the way Havelange, Blatter, Grondona, and their gang offered me so many years ago. No way. "The family" stinks of the mafia, and that's what FIFA was. I would have liked to be part of a FIFA where, if I went out to dinner, I wouldn't pay with the FIFA credit card— that would be using soccer money to chow down with my friends. That would be stealing. And that's exactly what they've been doing all this time, and I hope it comes to an end. Are we all nuts? They say that players can't run the league because we don't have the authority. But who would we learn from? Just the way an old shoemaker chooses a kid to learn the trade, Blatter chose Platini at a certain point, not to learn how to run things, but to learn how to work the system.

There's a lot of stuff that still has to be worked out at FIFA, and in the federations too. The anti-doping tests, for example—something I have some personal experience with and I'll say so before anyone else has a chance to. You know what should be done? The anti-doping test should be about prevention, not punishment. And the tests should be performed better too, which means not letting anyone meddle with them—not the sporting brands or anyone, because some of the brands get involved to keep the careers of their stars from crashing down. That's not prevention, that's cover-up. Prevention means not punishing a player the first time he tests positive, or even the second time. If he keeps using, put him in rehab, but don't suspend him. If he can't keep playing, help him find a purpose in life. Help the person recover, even if the player can't.

One more thing: no more choosing the hosts of two World Cups at the same time. Enough of that. Isn't it obvious that it's only a way to get more votes and more money from bribes? From now on, they should just go over the options and choose the host for the next cup. End of story.

But judging from the last FIFA elections, there doesn't seem to be much of a move to make changes. They elected Gianni Infantino, who went from picking out the hot and cold balls during the draws to being president of FIFA. Did he care that his boss, Blatter, was against the ropes or might even have gone behind bars? Did he really care about soccer? These questions should go to the prosecutor who is investigating the whole thing: shouldn't Infantino be summoned? Let me just remind you, with all due respect, that he was Platini's assistant for nine years.

CHAPTER 6

Crossing the Río de la Plata in Mexico

ARGENTINA 1, URUGUAY 0
—Puebla, Monday, June 16

Of all the games in the cup, my best by far was the game against Uruguay. First, because I never once lost possession when challenged by a defender; I beat out every Uruguayan player they put before me. They didn't see me once on their side of the field—not once—and that was key. In one of our run-ins on the field—I am not sure which one of us was downfield—I even heard Enzo Francescoli say to the Uruguayan defenders, "Do whatever you have to do to stop him. I don't care if it means grabbing him by the jersey!" Just like that. Enzo is amazing. We got along even back then. But it was an Argentina-Uruguay matchup, and in an Argentina-Uruguay matchup, you're grinding your teeth and not giving anything away.

URUGUAYANS WILL BE URUGUAYANS

They had barely made it to the round of sixteen. They had played well against Germany at the opening match, but then struggled against the Danes, who were killer, with Elkjaer Larsen (I knew him well from Verona) and Michael Laudrup, who was just a kid of twenty-two but already ripping it up over there at Juve; they had Morten Olsen, a great defender, and Søren Lerby, who "El Flaco" Menotti predicted was going to shine at the cup. A powerful team. The Danes' second game was against Uruguay and they scored six goals against them—that's right, six! Then the Yoruguas tied Scotland, zero to zero, and managed to qualify by the skin of their teeth, by just two points. They came in as one of the best of the third-ranked teams—counting goals, with two fewer goals scored against them than Hungary. That game against the Scots was one of the few we went to the stadium to see, because it was played at Neza stadium, near Mexico City.

We had made it to the round of sixteen, so the time had come to take a look around, to see how the other guys were playing.

I think the Latin American teams had done a better job at overcoming the obstacles: the altitude, the weather, the field conditions. We were used to that sort of thing. And, just like the Danes, the Brazilians were at the top of their game. They were the only two teams that didn't lose a single point in the first round. The Brazilian coach was Telê Santana, and they had some great players: Zico would sub in, but as starters were Sócrates, Careca, Alemão, Júnior. The other team that qualified from their group was Spain, but they were not yet playing to their full potential. They had trouble beating Algeria, a team with players who knew what to do with a ball, like Madjer and Belloumi. They demolished Northern Ireland with two goals by my friend Careca—who was not yet my friend. For those who believed the hype, Algeria had the cup in the bag. All the better for us if they didn't see us coming.

Mexico was the home team and they had Hugo Sánchez, who was a star at Real Madrid, but they still had trouble making it to the knockout round. I think Hugo was probably the best player Mexico ever had, but they still had trouble on the home field. Their coach was Bora "El Loco" Milutinovic—a real character. The other teams to qualify from that group were Paraguay (another South American team, see what I mean?) and Belgium, which was working its way up slowly but surely.

Just like the Soviets—it was still the USSR back then—who had a great goalie in Dasayev and a good playmaker in Belanov. They would attack like you couldn't believe. They ended up with a better score than France in their group. And France wasn't just Platini. It was also Amoros, Tigana, Giresse, Luis Fernández, Papin . . . But they had trouble advancing to the knockout stage at the cup, a lot of trouble.

We, on the other hand, had been doing very well, but we could have been even better. We had beaten the Koreans, three to nothing, in the first game; then we tied Italy, one to one, but we played great; and we had smeared the Bulgarians in the last game. I mean, we only beat them two to nothing, but we should have kept the pressure up—I was pissed that we hadn't. I wanted to beat everyone. Every last team.

We finished first in our group, group A, with five points. Undefeated. Undefeated! We scored six goals and only two had been scored against us.

Against the Uruguayans, it was Pumpido, Cuciuffo, Brown, Ruggeri, and Garré; Valdano and Pasculli; and Giusti,

Burruchaga, Batista, and me. Write that lineup down, because it would be the last time we played in that formation. I remember saying to the guys, "Don't get too cocky. Don't get too cocky. They have some good players who would kill to bring us down." And, I went on and on, "We have to stay focused. We haven't won anything yet."

That doesn't mean I wasn't brimming with self-confidence. Especially after what we had been able to do against Italy, I was convinced that we would go far. But Uruguayans will be Uruguayans. I remembered '79, first the South American Youth Soccer Championship in Montevideo, and then the FIFA World Youth Championship in Japan.

In Montevideo, they beat us and took the title: we lost to them in round one and then they beat us, one to nothing, in the final. It was really rough in Tokyo, though. They were brutal, but we won the game and made it to the final. I remember that game perfectly because it was so rough—they really lit into us! The goalie for that team was Alvez, and there were also Bossio, Barrios, and Rubén Paz, who kicked ass. And those were the guys we would be up against in Mexico. The rivalry against Uruguay is timeless.

IT SHOULD HAVE BEEN FOUR TO NOTHING

We took a bus from the training camp, in Mexico City, near Azteca stadium, to Puebla, where we had played against Italy. It was just over ninety miles, and it took us less than two hours. We knew the roads—and the rituals—well. Each player knew where he had to sit. We troublemakers sat in the middle.

I remember that Valdano was staring out the window,

because we drove through so many different kinds of neigh-
borhoods. Some of them had unbelievably luxurious homes;
others were very poor, with people sitting on the sidewalk
cutting hair. It was like taking a tour of all Mexico in a few
hours.

I don't know what it's like now, but the other day, when I
was watching the reopening of Cuauhtémoc stadium on TV—
Boca Juniors was playing in that opening game—I could
barely recognize it. Thirty years ago, it had the capacity to
hold thirty thousand people, and the day we played against
Uruguay it wasn't full. And the crowd was divided—more
people rooting for Argentina than for Uruguay—but we
didn't yet feel any hostility from the Mexicans. There were a
bunch of Argentine fans. There were hooligans too, but only
the ones for Boca, with José "El Abuelo" Barrita at the head.
They did go to the camp, but they never got beyond the
gate. They never once came in.

One time, I remember that we were going on our usual
outing to the mall, and they were outside, blocking the gate—
El Abuelo and a few other guys from Boca. They asked us for
some dough. They were staying at a house somewhere—I'm
not sure where. The guys on the team talked about what to
do, the way we talked about everything. We decided not to
give them anything—and we didn't. I think there might have
been some hooligans from the Chacarita club there too—but
all in all, there were no more than fifty guys. They never
bothered us, and I don't think they bothered anyone else either. Times were different—you know what I'm saying?

What I do remember perfectly was how hot it was when
we started playing against Uruguay—during all the games
we played at the cup, really. And at the end there was a huge

thunderstorm. But what I remember most of all was that we blew them away.

I recently rewatched this game for the first time too, just to reconfirm what I already thought: we almost scored four or five times, or my name isn't Diego Armando Maradona. We had some trouble in the last few minutes, it's true, because we didn't follow through on certain plays. But that game should have ended four to nothing or, at the least, four to one.

Check it out . . .

Who was our right fullback? Cuciuffo, that's right. So why did he turn up on the left in the second play of the game? See what I'm saying? Check out the game again and you'll see that in the first play Cuciuffo plays on the right and then turns up on the left. See what I mean when I say we didn't have any set order?

It's true that Cuciuffo had to keep Francescoli under control and so he followed him. Garré was a lot less mobile and had more trouble attacking. Batista and Giusti saw to recovering the ball at midfield, and Burruchaga, Valdano, Pasculli, and I were on the move the whole time. Any one of us could move center. Behind, everything went smoothly thanks to the wisdom of "El Cabezón" Ruggeri and "Tata" Brown—that wisdom straightened out situations in the game that could have cost us dearly.

Check out El Cabezón. He was great—so fast, so gutsy, so agile. We all felt more and more confident with each passing game. Now, when I watch it again, I realize that I never once lost the ball in a face-off. Not once.

There was a lot of talk during the game, as you might imagine, it being Uruguay and all. Besides, they were really fired up. But it wasn't a violent game, not at all. There was a rumor that before the game Barrios or Bossio—I'm not sure which—came up to me to tell me to rest assured they weren't going to go after me. That never happened. Nobody said anything like that to me, because that would have gone against the spirit of the Uruguayan player. There was some contact, of course, but nothing out of the ordinary. They came out to get me a few times, and when Uruguayans kick you, they mean it. When they go for your ankle, it hurts. Some guys might step on your foot, but a Uruguayan will straight-out hack at you. No beating around the bush.

They put Barrios on me, though it also could have been Bossio. But it was Barrios. And what I did was make him run from one side of the field to the other, from left to right and back again. And it was there, on the left, that he had to kick me a few times to stop me.

Not five minutes in and I had already shown him—and myself—that the best strategy would be to break away on the left. I had one on the right but ended up against the advertising boards. But then I broke past on the left, dragging Barrios behind me. And I kicked center from the left wing, one of those moves I love so much: squeezed between the end line and the defender, I would tear down the field and hook the ball, almost spooning it, but powerfully. Like that time. The play ended in a corner kick, but it was a sign. Barrios was a big guy, much taller than me, which is why once I got going he couldn't catch up.

Right away we had our first almost-goal. Alvez kicked it long from the goal, and Batista brought it back upfield. The ball went past "El Tano" Gutiérrez, and I went up the left side, almost inside the penalty area, and kicked it center to reach Valdano, who was on his way there. Jorge went for a diving header, but he only managed to nick the ball, and it went out of bounds. That was, for me, our first almost-goal. But you better keep track because there are a bunch more coming.

Valdano was there doing his best for both our offense and our defense. He experienced the whole Bilardo versus Menotti thing the same way I did: we put that all aside to play for Argentina.

During that first half, the Uruguayans never, or almost never, made it into our area. Nery had no trouble blocking a center by Venancio Ramos. And ten minutes after that first shot by Valdano, I took one. A free kick that knocked the hell out of the crossbar. I used to love it when my foot would hit the ball full on. When that happens, you don't have to see how it turns out: you know as soon as it comes off your foot that it might well be a goal. It wasn't that time, but it missed by just an inch.

The secret is to leave your foot on the ball for a little while, to stay with it as long as you can. If not, the ball doesn't know where you want it to go. Once, when I was the coach of the Argentine team, I told Messi just that. If you don't believe me, just ask Fernando Signorini. El Ciego told the story in a book he wrote, because he was there to witness it in Marseilles. It was the practice before a friendly against the French, and Lio Messi—along with Mascherano and someone else—stayed on awhile practicing free kicks. He kicked it into the stands once. Annoyed, because he doesn't like losing at anything, he headed for the locker room. Fernando gave him a hard time. "You're heading off now, after such a crappy kick?" And Lio came back. I had seen the whole thing and I gestured for Lio to stay with me. I kicked the ball just so—keeping my foot on it—and explained it to Messi, who got it immediately.

That evening in Puebla, against the Uruguayans, I was just an inch off; I should have left my foot on the ball a second more.

IT FINALLY WENT IN

So far two almost-goals—start keeping track. We played better and better as the game progressed, and the same was true of the cup as a whole: minute by minute we got better. I was so proud. And not even my daughter Dalma could fit into those little shorts I wore. What players wear now is like a skirt compared to what we had to wear. I was so thin! And so fast . . . I even had time to run downfield to recover the ball and everything. Sure, but that was thirty years ago.

At around halfway into the first half, Barrios played dirty on me for the first time. He ran right into me, hitting me above and below the waist, and stuck his hand in my face for good measure. I got another free kick but I didn't keep my foot on the ball long enough, and it flew over the net. The one who tried to make it up to me later was Barrios, apologizing and all. It was all good; we were like perfect little ladies.

But there were a few rough run-ins and, in one of them—or, actually, in two, one right after the other—Garré was kicked out of the game. Francescoli flicked the ball past him, and Garré slammed into him. A minute later, same thing. Luigi Agnolin gave him a yellow card, which would mean that Garré couldn't play in the next game—if we qualified, that is, because this game was still tied at zero.

But sometimes that's how history is written. If Garré

hadn't gotten the yellow card, "El Vasco" Olarticoechea would not have been put in the game. In that game, we realized just how much talent we had on the bench. Absolutely! I mean, we were already in the round of sixteen and El Vasco hadn't been a starter in a single game, even though he was in amazing, and I mean amazing, shape.

At the end of the first period, El Vasco had another breakaway on the left, and "El Tano" Gutiérrez almost scored an own goal against Alvez. Until then, the stars had been "Checho" Batista, Ruggeri, and Brown, not because Uruguay was getting close to our goal much—they almost never did—but because we were always anticipating what play they would make. All we had to do was get it in the net—that was it. The rest was in place. And, in the end, we did it.

At the forty-two minute mark, when it seemed like the first half was over, we started out from way downfield. I faked out Barrios twice, then looked for Batista, who fell over as he passed off to the side to Burruchaga. Burru sent the ball into the penalty area, it rebounded off of Valdano, and poor Acevedo ran right into the ball and knocked it center. It was the best assist Pasculli could have imagined. Pasculli didn't even ask who had passed him the ball. He kicked straight away with his right foot, crossing the ball to the far goalpost. The truth is, we deserved it: the third clear shot had to end in goal.

I was happy for Pasculli. I was the one who had insisted that we buy Pedrito to play with Argentinos Juniors. For $120,000, I remember it was! Miguel Ángel López was the coach at that time. We gave the team Pasculli was playing for, Colón de Santa Fe, like twenty checks for $15,000. That's why I had a warm spot for Pasculli. Besides, we roomed together. I saw him in good times and in bad. Because after that game, Bilardo benched him for good. I was the one who had to put up with him crying over it. It's true, if he hadn't made the change, I would have had to put up with Héctor.

Enrique, who said he was going to go home if he didn't play. Enrique also had a strong personality. I wasn't surprised that he made the team. Others were, but not me. I knew he was a great player, with something to offer in every play even though he had only played one game with the team.

He ended up being really important because he was there for all of us whenever we needed him on the field. Bilardo was always ranting about the importance of hard work, which is why he put Enrique on the team even though he had barely played any games. Bilardo had him in Toulon, but he hardly put him in. Then he was added to the roster.

For many, he ended up being one of the surprises at the cup. In that game against Uruguay, Bilardo had him warming up in the locker room—along with "El Vasco" Olarticoechea—starting at halftime. Enrique told me so himself last Christmas, which he spent at my place. He spent the whole time warming up, but Bilardo never put him in. He sent El Vasco in and told him to play more upfield, to see how that went. He put Olarticoechea in, but not Enrique, which is why Enrique never thought he would play in the next game—if we made it. He had no idea what was in store for him.

But the biggest surprise, the great revelation, was "El Tata" Brown, especially since he was under so much pressure as the one who replaced Passarella, who had jumped ship. El Tata was amazing, a real superstar on defense, and at keeping control of the ball, which he had never done in his whole goddamn life. I think this was the high point of his career; he never played like that again—and it's to his credit that he did it there. There are World Cup players, just as there are extremely talented guys who do great for their clubs or even in the qualifiers but freeze up at the World Cup.

And then, in the second half, my show began. Right away, I put the pressure on and Agnolin called a foul for a studs-up tackle that I hadn't committed. But just two minutes in, we mounted a counterattack, and I sprinted up the right side. "El Gringo" Giusti sent a long pass my way—I tapped it past "El Tano" Gutiérrez and avoided his attempt at foul play. I came up against Bossio and got past him—I told you my show was about to begin. From the right, I put a curl on the ball with my left foot, holding my body steady to keep the ball nice and tight. When you kick the ball straight, there's the risk that the guy who comes to block the shot might throw you to the ground. If you put a curl on it, though, you open up to one side and the defender can't make it—the goalie either. It's a way to get fewer players between you and the goal.

Now they call it "ball control," but it's nothing new.

Anyway, I put a curl on it to get around Alvez, and it ended up with Pasculli in front of the net. He shot, but it went out past the far goalpost. Another almost-goal . . . Three so far, plus the goal, right? Valdano's head shot, my free kick into the crossbar.

There would be more—plenty more—in the second period.

AND THEY STARTED LIGHTING INTO US

A free kick by "El Flaco" Francescoli caused Nery a little trouble—not much, just a little. And then we had another almost-goal. I was able to get rid of Barrios at midfield, which meant we had an edge, a clearer playing field. I fell over as I passed the ball to Pasculli, who broke away on the left and kicked a center straight toward the box just as Burruchaga was arriving. Burru kicked it twice, but the ball didn't make it in. One more, and now it's four, plus the goal.

We were so confident that even "El Gringo" Giusti tried a few shots from outside the box. Sure, they ended up in the stands, but he made a shot. He even stole one of my free kicks. He kicked it and it went long. "You'll never do a free kick again with me on the field, Gringo, as long as you live," I told him.

I stayed farther upfield, on the left, which was where I could cause Bossio more trouble. I didn't want us to be on the counterattack and, the truth is, we weren't. We always started putting the pressure on from way upfield, and our confidence was growing. I had another attempt, after a sweet pass from Burruchaga. I kicked it long range, but Alvez saved it. I'm not saying it was the greatest attempt on the goal we had, but you can add it to the list. By this point, fifteen minutes into the second period, we were clearly outplaying Uruguay.

Argentina wasn't being cautious any longer, because we players didn't want to be. Uruguay was being cautious, and even though they were losing, they didn't go on the offensive. If you watch the game, the way I did, some thirty years later, you can see that we had to take the initiative in that game. Look at the way I marked my guy, always focused on getting the ball back. You'll see that we were always gathering at midfield because we knew to start passing there. What "Checho" Batista, Burruchaga, and I did was distract them and take the ball away. That was because there were so many of us at the midfield. And you can really see that in the next game, when Pasculli was taken out and Enrique put in. That was when we started winning the World Cup at midfield.

This was when the Uruguayans started lighting into us more. Barrios went after me, and after Pasculli. And the referee, Agnolin, who had given Garré and Brown warnings, played dumb. They tripped me twice in one minute, and he didn't say anything. They might not have done it as glaringly as the Koreans, but they did foul plenty in the second period. And I mean plenty. Some parts of my body hurt more than others—like my back, that hurt much more than the blows to my ankles or my knees. But I had Carmando, who could work magic. Magic hands. He would massage me before and after each game. When he rubbed me down in the locker room before a game, I might fall—no matter how important the game was. He relaxed me completely. He used a strange rub with mud in it. He never told me what it was, and I never asked.

They quickly put Rubén Paz in for Acevedo. Everyone thought that was going to cause us some trouble, but not at all! He managed to break away on the left side a few times as soon as he started playing, but he didn't come anywhere near the goal. Not once.

We, on the other hand, did make it all the way. Once again, starting at midfield. Looking back on the cup, I notice a few things: stepping on the gas pedal from there, just past the midfield line, would do the other team in. That, combined with my short sprints, made a huge difference. I played with Valdano, who went straight for Alvez. He shot the ball down the right side, and the goalie came out to catch it. It rebounded off, to me, with "El Tano" Gutiérrez closing in. I beat him to it and scored with an instep drive.

But Agnolin disqualified that goal. Foul. He called a foul! There was no way it was a foul. My foot came down sideways. I complained about it in Italian. And, some time later, I ran into him at an Italian tournament. A Napoli-Roma game, I remember it was. I went up to him and said, "That was some sweet goal you stole from me—you know?"

"You know something, Diego? I looked at it later and you're right."

"What good does it do me to be right, you motherfucker!" I screamed at him.

"I thought it was a studs-up tackle, Diego. And it wasn't. You took the ball and kicked it like . . ."

I never, ever, lift up my foot. Too bad. We would have brought the game to an end at that point. I've already lost count of all the almost-goals.

I kept complaining. In Italian I swore to him on my entire family that it had not been a studs-up tackle. But, meanwhile, we kept making our way to their goal. Burruchaga made this great center that Valdano, on the other side, headed and "El Tano" Gutiérrez kicked out of play. I kept after Agnolin.

There were fifteen minutes left, but instead of the Uruguayans trying to take us by storm at the ninth hour, as you might have expected, a real storm came. It was raining like mad! First gusts of wind and then buckets of rain. Terrible. Our blue jerseys started weighing us down like sweaters, and it wasn't the symbolic weight of the Argentine jersey; it was because they were heavy with rain.

Barrios had to take me down twice—twice in the same way—for Agnolin to give him a warning. It was on the left side, almost at the wing, where we were driving them crazy with our counterattacks.

When I compare the game against Korea with the game against Uruguay, it seems more like two completely different cups than two different games! We were really fast this game, much faster than against Korea or Bulgaria. That happens sometimes at World Cups. Things speed up. Besides, the players get more self-confident. They have a special motivation.

And then there's the fear factor.

I liked it, because that's how World Cups are played. You have to be eager, to feel your best, to feel important, to know you're representing your country. And we still hadn't earned the respect of all our naysayers. By no means. But we were already preparing the song, "This one is for you / all you / motherfuckers." Who were the motherfuckers? All the journalists. Mostly the journalists, actually.

DO OR DIE

It was just three minutes from the end of the game when Uruguay did that famous play that made everyone think they had us on the ropes, which was not true. It was almost a goal, though—it's true. The ball fell short of Cuciuffo just outside the area, and Rubén Paz gave it a beautiful kick with his left foot. It was pouring and the grass was slippery. Nery Pumpido hurled himself on the ball, but it stayed in the box. "El Flaco" Francescoli gave it his all, feetfirst, slide-tackling Nery and slamming right into him. And what for? That's all I want to know! I was really fond of "El Flaco" Francescoli—we had even been chatting before the game—but we both wanted to win, of course. We gave it our all. And he got along even better with the members of the Argentine team who were teammates of his at River Plate. But I remember that Ruggeri went right over to confront him, almost picking him up by the nape of his neck! Valdano and Brown also came tearing downfield to join the fray. I mean, there was no time left, and at this point we would do anything to run out the clock. There was no way they could get away from us. It was do or die. It was a good game, real good.

When Nery stood up—about a century later—we sprinted upfield. Pumpido stood there with us. It wasn't breathtaking. It wasn't something that would save a game, but it wouldn't ruin it either. The national team's goalie. The thing is, we had one more play—the last one of the game—with less than a minute left. I got the ball at midfield, did that spin I always used to do, and then saw a player in blue go by me. And I passed it ahead knowing that there was nobody behind me. The player was Pedrito Pasculli. I passed him the ball, and he started dribbling and went one-on-one against Alvez. He kept going—he couldn't help himself—and Alvez ended up getting rid of him. I was as fast as a jet plane back then. See how I flicked it? I spotted Pasculli and, whop, just like that . . .

That was how the game ended, with us trying to score one more time. That's why I say that we had a lot of chances in the second period. Pedro, Valdano, Burruchaga, me, Valdano again—we all made it down there. Plus Pedro's goal. So the game could have ended five to nothing. Uruguay couldn't do anything to us—they didn't even get a shot on goal until the last fifteen minutes of the game. After that, it was all in our favor, and Rubén Paz didn't end up mattering so much. Still, it's a good thing they didn't put him in sooner. But it was our fault we did not score more, not a question of what Uruguay did.

Take another look at the game if you can, and you'll see that it was our fault—not the rain's or Uruguay's—that it ended one to nothing. It should have been five or six to nothing. Seriously. Because we played seriously.

And we celebrated seriously that evening too. We were going nuts. We knew that we were playing better and better, that we were quick as jet planes. But, at that point, the only planes were the ones flying overhead to take the other guys home. We were staying on in Mexico.

CHAPTER 7

A Final of Sorts

ARGENTINA 2, ENGLAND 1
—Mexico City, Sunday, June 22

If it had been up to the Argentines, each of us, the players would have gone out there with a machine gun and killed Shilton, Stevens, Butcher, Fenwick, Sansom, Steven, Hodge, Reid, Hoddle, Beardsley, and Lineker. But we didn't want to get involved in that whole mess. They were our rivals on the field—that was it. I did want to shoot some things their way, like hat tricks and nutmegs. I wanted to dance around them, score a goal with my hand, and then score another one, the second one, which would become the greatest goal in soccer history.

I remember it well. When the press found out that we were going to play England in the quarterfinals, we didn't comment; we knew they would ask about what goal celebrations we were planning, whether we were going to give Thatcher the finger, whether we would punch Shilton. We knew the story, which is why we chose to steer clear, to keep calm. In any case, we internalized the whole thing. But I can assure you, I was burning up inside. My heart almost pounded its way clear out of my chest. But we had to play that match.

During the buildup to the game, everyone had the Falklands War on their mind. How could they not? The truth is that the English had killed a bunch of kids. They were guilty, but the Argentines were just as guilty, sending those kids out in Flecha tennis shoes to fight against the world's third-largest military power. You never lose your sense of patriotism, but wanting a war is something else entirely. And if there had to be a war, at least we could have won it. I remember well when we got to Spain in '82 and saw the first uncensored coverage of the war: it was a massacre, a pile of legs and arms, of all those Argentine boys snuffed out in the Malvinas (the Falkland Islands), while those military sons of bitches in Argentina kept telling us we were winning the war.

I remembered that perfectly well, so I didn't play that game thinking we were going to win the war. All I wanted to do was honor the memory of the dead, to give the families of those boys some relief, and to wipe England off the world map—the world soccer map, that is. Eliminating them from the World Cup in the quarterfinals was like forcing them to surrender.

It was a battle, oh yes, but on my battlefield.

I can't blame Lineker. No, no, no, boys. What we had was a soccer match, and that's the way we all saw it. Because the English guys treated us like gentlemen. Even after we won, they came over to congratulate us, coming into the locker room to swap jerseys. I mean, I'm sometimes made out to be an enemy of England or something, but I'm not their enemy. I think it's really moving that the English remember Bobby Charlton, say, seventy years after he last stepped on the field.

But, unfortunately, I don't think that will ever happen in Argentina. Take "El Tata" Brown, champion of the world: one afternoon a few years back they wouldn't even let him into the Estudiantes stadium. All this is what we were talking about at the training camp before we went out. It's true it wasn't just another game: how could it have been? From the moment we knew we were going to be playing England, we couldn't think of anything else. We had gone to Azteca stadium to see them play against Paraguay. They beat the Paraguayans easily. I wasn't surprised they had made it to the quarterfinals: they were the better team.

We were scheduled to play the English in that same stadium—our first game there—at noon. It was just five minutes away from the training camp, and the bus was going to leave for the stadium at nine thirty in the morning. But at nine o'clock, half an hour early, we were all ready to go, lined up like soldiers. Even though I always sleep like a baby, I had woken up earlier than ever. I wanted the game to start. I wanted to go out there and play and put an end to all the talk.

And, in the locker room, we kept at it. We were focused on one thing and one thing only: how we were going to play that game. We had lost a war to them, it's true, but that wasn't our fault or the fault of the guys we were going to play against. And that knowledge gave us the energy we needed.

That's what I talked to the boys about. Because we were all fired up, really fired up. We did our rituals, like we had for the previous games. I would draw a player on the floor before Carmando wrapped me up. And woe to anyone who stepped on it. Our Lady of Luján was right where she was supposed to be; everything was in place.

There's a picture I always remember, a really great, special shot: the two teams are walking into the stadium, down some sort of ramp installed behind an arch. There were 115,000 people in the stands, but all I could hear was the clicking of our cleats on that metallic floor. There was no more talking at that point, not between us players or to any of them.

We had already greeted them because there was a room where the players from both teams could get together before each game. I had played Osvaldo Ardiles's testimonial game with Glenn Hoddle, wearing the Tottenham jersey, and I got along with him just fine. The English were taking the whole thing very seriously and behaved with the utmost respect, which was just the way it should have been. We were just as serious and respectful.

It was hard for them too. We found out that before the game some guy had gone in to talk to them—the minister of sport or something like that—to tell them to watch what they said to journalists and not to let themselves get carried away in the heat of the game. So we were all in the same boat.

The energy was out there, with the people, the fans, doing their part.

But the fans were mostly there to see a soccer game. The whole political affair had been played out someplace else, between the people and their governments, not between the players. Politicians have always used soccer and they always will, no question about that. Taking a picture of yourself with a *pato* player isn't the same as with a soccer player—and politicians know that, and that's not going to change. And winning the World Cup makes a difference, having a national team win the cup calms things down.

Nowadays, I get along just fine with the English. We get

along, I should say, because every time Diego Maradona—or Dalma or Gianinna Maradona—lands in England and shows a passport at the immigration desk, they say, "You're a legend." I really like how the English have changed, how they went from having brutal hooligans who would kill people to being what they are today. Now you can go and sit down in the Newcastle stands wearing an Arsenal jersey and it's all good.

And speaking of jerseys, the story of the blue jersey we wore in that match against England is very special, very special indeed.

A SPECIAL JERSEY FOR A SPECIAL MATCH

Le Coq Sportif had made us a really nice home jersey. The fabric was eyelet, a light mesh that was ideal for the terrible heat in Mexico, especially at noon, an unbearable hour. But they had forgotten that we also had to have an alternate jersey—I don't think they cared much about that. When we played against Uruguay in Puebla, it started pouring and the alternate blue jersey they had given us weighed us down like a wet sweater. When we found out that we were going to have to wear that alternate jersey against England because they were wearing white, we got really upset: playing a match at that altitude in Mexico City at noon in a sweater? And against England? No way!

We asked the brand to make us a blue one in eyelet, just like the home jersey, but they said they couldn't do it in time for the match. Bilardo took out a pair of scissors and started punching little holes in the blue jerseys to try to imitate eyelet—totally ludicrous.

But poor Rubén Moschella, the AFA office employee, was able to work it out. He was the one who had gotten me the list of the phone numbers that allowed me to figure out how much Passarella had spent on phone calls, so why wouldn't he be able to come up with a set of blue jerseys? It seems like a joke now, but it was a real problem back then. I mean, could anyone imagine a national team at the World Cup today combing the city looking for an alternate jersey, as if they were in Once, the Buenos Aires neighborhood where fabrics are sold? Well, that's exactly what we did.

Moschella went to forty different stores. Forty. Some say he went to Héctor Zelada's shop—Zelada played for Argentina, but he also had a sporting goods store—but Zelada doesn't remember it. The one thing for sure is that Moschella found two jerseys at two different stores. But neither was eyelet; that was a special design. He asked them to put both models on hold and came by the training camp with them to ask which one he should buy. He could have just bought both sets, but that's how they pinched pennies back then!

So there they were, checking out both models, one day before the game. They asked me, and I didn't hesitate for a second. I pointed to one of them and said, "That one. We'll beat England in that one."

Naturally, "that one" was missing the national team emblem and the numbers—just a minor detail. Two seamstresses at the training camp sewed them on. They did a pretty good job but missed a few details, like the laurel leaves.

And the numbers, the numbers were a joke. When we went out onto the field, some of the guys had sparkles on their face because the numbers were silver and sparkly. And after genius kit man Tito Benrós had ironed those numbers onto thirty-eight jerseys, he looked like he should have been at carnival, not at Azteca stadium! If it happened to rain, like it had in our match against Uruguay, it was going to be a real disaster: we wouldn't know who was who or what position the others were playing.

So with our hands and faces covered in sparkles, we went to sleep at eleven o'clock that night. And the game was early the next morning.

NOT ONE STEP BACK

But the whole thing with the jerseys wasn't the only source of tension in the days before the match.

As if playing against England weren't enough, Bilardo came looking for me in the room I was sharing with Pedro Pasculli. It was weird because he asked me to come out and talk to him. But when I heard what he had to say, it made perfect sense.

"Diego, I'm pulling Pasculli out . . ."

I didn't say a word.

"I'm taking the chance."

"It's up to you," I answered. "The one thing I can tell you is that you'll be destroying that man in there, the man who scored the winning goal against Uruguay."

"Yeah, but these guys are going to blow right past him."

The only thing that mattered to me was consoling Pedro, who cried like a baby. And my only consolation was that Enrique, a powerhouse, would be playing—a guy who had forced Bilardo to make a change on the merits of his game, a guy Bilardo had been forced to call even though he had barely played for the national team, and one who forced his hand again now because his personality had made him part of our team.

The other guy who was in was "El Vasco" Olarticoechea. In my opinion, he was the ace of spades. He had never been a starter before. But physically, it was clear that he had totally adapted to the altitude. Every time he had come in as a substitute, he had played a mean game—torn the ball apart. El Vasco came in for Garré, who had reached the maximum number of fouls during the game against Uruguay. If it hadn't been for him, I don't know who would have played—I really don't know. I don't want to repeat myself, but Bilardo claims that all those talks we would have lasted an hour, but that's a lie; they lasted twenty minutes, max. And some things just happened without any discussion. Take Enrique, for example. He had no idea he was going to play that game. Not a clue. He didn't find out until the day of the game. And you know something else about Enrique? He didn't have cleats; no brand had given him cleats. I got Puma to sponsor him so he could play in the World Cup. You tell me if that could happen to a player today. Even the boys who play for the youth soccer leagues in Argentina have cleats the brand gives them!

Enrique coming in meant a tactical change, and that allowed us to block well over half the field, with Burruchaga on the wing, backed by Giusti, who was also on that side. Enrique was on the other side of the field, with Olarticoechea behind him. And "El Checho" Batista was the center midfielder. Downfield, Brown was our sweeper, with Cuciuffo and Ruggeri as stoppers. And upfield, Valdano, who would come back down if needed, and me.

The historic lineup, Bilardo's tactical revolution, the one

everyone remembers, happened in the quarterfinals. Until then, we had played with four defenders, no screwing around.

This was a smart team, a team that played against each rival the way the rival had to be played. No team played at our level, let alone outplayed us. On the contrary: except for a few minutes toward the end of the game against England, no one took us by surprise.

We had watched the English beat Paraguay, three to zilch. We knew they played the midfield well, we knew they were fierce, and we knew they weren't kids: they were men with experience. Going back over their lineup, you can see I was right: Shilton, Stevens, Sansom, Fenwick, and Butcher; Hoddle, Reid, Steven, and Hodge; Lineker and Beardsley.

I already knew Hoddle, and I thought he was a player you had to be careful with. He kicked well with both feet; he was the one who pulled the team together. He and Beardsley, who got in on every play. We talked about this with Bilardo as well. One player we didn't expect was Barnes, who came in as a substitute and made our lives difficult. Every time I see him—and I've seen him plenty of times at Champions games in England and in Dubai too (he's a little on the chubby side, like me)—he bursts out laughing, as if to say, "Boy, I sure scared the shit out of you guys!"

And, it's true, Barnes did scare the shit out of us, but that was toward the end. We started out the match on our own terms. I admit it, the war was on our mind, even though we had done our best to avoid it. All that stuff about the war . . . In the first half, we were a little nervous. It took us forty-five minutes to make sense of it.

Our previous game had been against Uruguay. And, like I

said, I thought that game was better, even the best game we played in the cup. I still think so. But, with no disrespect to Uruguay, we were up against England. And I was convinced that England was one step above Uruguay. Why? Not because I had more respect for them as players. We had started down a path with that victory against Uruguay and we couldn't take one step back—we couldn't! We had to keep pushing forward. If you ask Valdano, he's got something to say about this too. At halftime, I said, "Boys, boys! Not one step back, not a single step back!" I felt like we were playing too defensively, and I didn't like that. Bilardo didn't say a word. Not a single word. Or maybe he did say, "You're right, Diego."

What did I notice? Several things. First, the turf was in awful condition. Just awful. Truth be told, though, it was better at that point than when we played the final. But still, it was pathetic. So, what about it? Well, we were used to it, maybe because we trained a lot more and it was easier for us to adapt to that field after playing on the little fields at the training camp.

The other thing was the heat. It was incredibly hot, but we were up for it. The English suffered from the heat a lot more than we did. They got worn out faster than we did too.

The most important thing, though, was the altitude. They had come from playing in Monterrey: flat land. We had played two games in Mexico City and, to top it off, that's where we were staying. We no longer felt like our chests were exploding. We felt like we were flying high.

They ended up knocking into us sometimes because their timing was off. But they didn't mean any harm. I had never watched the full game until recently, and watching it confirmed what I felt back then: we all stuck to the rules. If you watch the match, you'll see that after the English kicked us, they would give us a hand to help us up. There wasn't any tremendous tension or anything that would indicate that something more than a game was at stake. We just took it one pass at a time.

Plus, man marking ended at that World Cup. I was always free to play, no matter what team they put on the field. I don't know whether Robson, the English coach, thought that assigning a guy to mark me would make things easier for me, but he didn't assign anyone. None of the English players marked me.

I was free to attack or to move downfield as far as I wanted. I would run them all the way down there, to midfield and a little farther even, because I knew I could narrow the angle a little more to make things easier on my teammates.

And so we were growing as a team, not when we trained, but during the games. I want people to understand that.

I was feeling better than ever at that point. I was flying! I would take the ball and speed dribble to stay seconds ahead of my opponents. I would stand on tiptoe and take off like Usain Bolt. Watching Bilardo's teams play bored me, but I was never bored playing on them, you know?

I never got bored because everyone passed me the ball. They knew I was the first choice, that they could always pass me the ball, no matter where I was or whom I was up against. Everyone had respect for us at that point. Even the referees. The Tunisian Ali Bennaceur was there, and he had watched the South Koreans and then the Uruguayans kick me.

I'm going to say it now, regardless of what happened later: less than ten minutes into the game, I made a run with the ball, my first one. I left two English players in the dust, and Fenwick knocked me down when I was reaching the penalty area. That's when the Tunisian came over and pulled out a yellow card. It was a sign, a good sign—everything, the play and the penalty card. Because later on I would make another run with the ball like that, and Fenwick would be one of the guys in my way. And I believe that yellow card taught him a lesson. That card allowed me to stake out the field, even though the play didn't lead to anything.

Afterward, "El Cabezón" Ruggeri headed a ball that sailed just over the crossbar, and, less than fifteen minutes in, Nery—who never failed, he was like clockwork—gave us our first scare. He wanted to come out dribbling, but since he's a goalie, he lost the ball. Beardsley, a player I really admired, stole the ball from him and came in from the side to take a shot. From midfield, I saw the ball flying toward the empty net and I said, "We're screwed." But we weren't: it landed outside the net.

I think that was one of the few shots they got. We set the pace and controlled the ball. It might not have been a very fun game to watch, but we were making clever moves, especially from the midfield on up. Downfield, the team was solid as a rock. "El Tata" Brown was no Kaiser: he was a marshal! As stoppers, Ruggeri and Cuciuffo were marking tight. And Giusti and "El Vasco" Olarticoechea were playing like clockwork. "El Gringo" Giusti even ventured into the penalty area because they still hadn't sent Barnes over to mark him. So he could play more as a midfielder, which came more naturally to him than being a winger (when he played on the wing, a turtle could get away from him). But during the first half, El Gringo even came up against Shilton, the goalie. He slipped and ended up crashing into him—which was really something. If it hadn't been the English, we might have ended up in a fistfight, like we almost did against the Uruguayans. But with the English, of all people, we ended up shaking hands, almost apologizing. Watching the match again confirms it. That's the way it went down.

People might not remember that, just like they don't remember that half an hour into the game I made a run like the one I would make later on, but that first one didn't end in a goal. It ended in a foul. Then I had a free kick that I should have aimed at the center of the net—I see that now—but it shaved the post. I wanted to get it in so bad. A goal—not cursing out the English—would be my revenge. On the next free kick, the ball bounced off the wall and out of bounds, so it was a corner kick for us, and that's when I got pissed off. Not at the English; I got pissed off at the corner flag. It was in my way, just like the photographers who were sitting there, and I pulled out the red flag and threw it down on the ground. I remember it so well: Ulloa, the assistant referee, came over to make me put the flag back in its place.

"Quit breaking my balls," I said to him. I was really ticked.

"I won't break your balls, but put the flag back where it goes," the guy answered.

"Okay, I'll put it back. And at the next World Cup, I'll be playing as a linesman."

The truth is, Ulloa was right. He could have carded me but he didn't. I put the flag on my head first and then I put it back on the pole. There's a nice picture of that.

Later I had another run, some sixty meters. I was in great shape, the best shape I've ever been in. I went right in for each attack and I knew they wouldn't be able to stop me. They either had to knock me down or I would keep on going, like when they elbowed me and the referee didn't see it. But, what the hell, what am I going to say about good old Bennaceur now, right? If not seeing this one meant not seeing that other one later on, all the better. The English guy did bump into me, it's true, but it wasn't intentional: he was turning just as I was getting up. That's why I didn't blame him for it. I did talk to him in my impeccable English—you can imagine—but what I said was that I understood what happened. The truth is, it was a gentlemen's match.

The English reached our penalty area once more during the first half, but just by kicking a few booters. They weren't playing creatively and we had control of the ball.

Just the same, I wasn't pleased. Having control was useless unless we scored. And we hadn't scored. That's why I said what I said in the locker room at halftime. Being in control of the game wasn't enough.

WHEN I SAY, "THE HAND OF GOD"

As soon as the second half started, I did what I always do, but this time for a special reason: I crossed myself. I kicked off with Valdano and we went to it. I didn't want to waste a second. I wanted to win this game no matter what. The time had come to change history.

Five minutes was all it took. Just five.

When after crossing half the field like a forward, "El Vasco" Olarticoechea passed me the ball—that was the great thing about him, he was a defender who handled the ball like a midfielder and attacked like a forward—I started moving upfield, controlling the ball, crossing on a diagonal from left to center, with the goal right between the eyes. It would be easy to get past them, I thought, because the English were all marking other players. I had my eye out for a blue jersey to do a wall pass—that was all I needed, because I knew that then I could go all the way on my own.

When I passed to Valdano, the ball bounced off him and went a little high, and Hodge was right next to him. So Hodge intercepted. But then Hodge made a mistake, which wasn't really a mistake, in my opinion, because you could still back-pass to the goalie then. What he did was volley it in Shilton's direction instead of trying to clear the ball. If Hodge had tried to clear it, the ball never would have come my way. Not ever.

But it floated down to me like a little balloon.

Oh boy, what a treat . . .

"This one is mine," I said. "I don't know if I'm going to make it, but I'll take my chances. If he calls a foul, he calls a foul." I leapfrogged, which was not what Shilton was expecting. I think he thought I was going straight for him. But I leapfrogged—check the pictures—you'll see the position my body was in.

I beat out Shilton because physically I was in the best shape of my life. He jumped, but I jumped before him, because I was watching the ball and he closed his eyes.

Shilton was used to hitting the ball with both fists and, as a result, he was sort of at a loss. If you look at the pictures, there's a huge space between Shilton, my hand, and the ball. You don't even see Shilton. And if you look at my feet, you'll see that I'm already in the air, moving upward. I keep moving up, and he hasn't even left the ground.

I say I leapfrogged because my legs were bent crosswise, like when you stretch your inner thighs. I was not even facing him. And you can see my ribs—I didn't have an ounce of fat—and how strong my legs are.

When I hit the ground, I went running to celebrate that goal. The ball had bounced in strong. I hit it with my fist, but it went in as if I had kicked it hard with my foot, not with my head. It hit the net and everything. It went straight in—bam!—and there was no way they could have seen it. Not the ref, not the linesman, not Shilton, who was in a daze, looking for the ball. The one who realized what happened was Fenwick, the last guy between me and the goal. But besides him, nothing, no one else. They all played it by ear, including Shilton, who didn't even know where he was standing.

I looked over at the referee, who hadn't yet made a call. I looked over at the linesman: same thing. And I went running off to celebrate. I decided on something they refused to acknowledge. Bennaceur, I later found out, looked at the linesman. And the linesman, a Bulgarian named Dotchev, didn't raise his flag or come running out into the middle of the field; he left it up to the ref. Afterward, they fought over who was responsible, blaming each other.

I kept on running, never looking back. "Checho" Batista was the first one to come over, but slowly, as if he were thinking, "They're not calling a foul—they're not calling it." I wanted the others to come over, but only Valdano and Burruchaga did. The thing is, Bilardo didn't let the midfielders celebrate the goals, because he didn't want them to get tired out. But this time I needed them—I really did.

I think they didn't want to look back toward the field, afraid that the goal would be disallowed. When El Checho came over, he asked me, "You knocked it in with your hand, right? Did you use your hand?"

And I answered, "Shut the fuck up and keep on celebrating."

Right then, I looked over at the stands, where my old man and Coco were watching. I lifted a closed fist in their direction, and they did the same thing back.

We were still afraid they would disallow the goal, but they didn't.

I am not sorry for scoring with my hand. Not sorry at all! With all due respect to the fans, the players, the management, I am not the least bit sorry. Because I grew up with this, because as a kid in Fiorito I would score goals with my hand all the time. And I did the same thing in front of a hundred thousand people, but no one saw it . . . because all they saw was the screaming after I had scored. And if they screamed that loud, it was because they were sure I had scored. So how could we possibly blame the Tunisian ref?

I won a lawsuit against an English newspaper that ran the story title, "Maradona says sorry," a thought that never once crossed my mind. Not then, not thirty years later . . . not on my deathbed. As I told a BBC reporter, one year later, "It was a totally legitimate goal, because the ref said it was good. I'm not one to doubt a ref's honesty, right?" I told Lineker the same thing, when he was at my house in Buenos Aires, doing another interview for a British TV channel.

The first thing he asked me was, "Did you make that goal with your hand, or was it the hand of God?"

And I answered, "It was my hand, but that doesn't mean I disrespect the English fans."

And I told him that I had made other goals that way, standing back to watch if the ref and his assistants took the bait. He realized it—he knew the deal like any soccer player would. He got why my teammates had run out to celebrate, though he also asked me about that. I told him I was the one who had called them to come embrace me, so no one would realize what had happened.

I remember him telling me that in England they would consider that play cheating, and whoever made a play like that a cheater. But I told him it was cunning, and whoever did it was clever.

That nice talk between two soccer players took place in the patio of my parents' house in Villa Devoto.

"So why did you say, 'the Hand of God'?" he asked me.

"Because God gave us a hand. He helped us out. Because the ref didn't see the play and the linesman didn't either—which is rare. That's why I said it was the hand of God."

"I blame the ref and the assistant, not you," he said. "And that second goal of yours was the first and only time in my career that I felt like applauding an opponent who made a goal against us."

I almost kissed him on the lips when he said that.

It was a dream goal. As soccer players, we always dream of making the goal of all goals. It's a dream we carry with us. And, the truth is, for me making that goal was fantastic. And in the World Cup, incredible!

"And was it even better that it was against England?" he asked, trying to get at me like a real journalist.

And I admitted that it was.

"It would have been much harder to make that goal against Italy, Uruguay, or Brazil. It was easier to get away with it because the English are more noble and honest on the field."

This guy wanted to go deeper, beyond the goals.

"A lot of people say you won the World Cup on your own. What do you say to that?"

"We had a great team. A great team that took shape with each game played. The foundation was the players' intelligence and, well, yeah . . . me being there was important—why should I say otherwise? I admit that."

I acknowledged back then—and I acknowledge today—that I didn't win the World Cup on my own. Without that team, we may have beaten England, but we wouldn't have won the cup.

Then he asked me again whether I felt bad about scoring with my hand, and I said that it was a game and that if the ref didn't call a foul, that was part of the game. And Lineker accepted that; he didn't say a word. Lineker is a great guy; that's the way we always talked whenever we saw each other.

Shilton, the goalie, was sure pissed though. And he still is. He said, "I won't invite Maradona to my testimonial match." Ha! And who would want to go to a goalie's testimonial match, let alone Shilton's? I mean, that guy's shock absorbers are worn out. Have you seen how he walks? Check it out, you'll see. New shock absorbers are what he needs.

And I made plenty of goals with my hand, plenty. For Cebollitas, for Argentinos, for Boca, for Napoli.

Playing for Cebollitas, I made a goal with my hand in Parque Saavedra. The other team spotted it and they went straight over to the ref. In the end, he allowed the goal and there was a big controversy. I knew it wasn't right, but it's one thing to look at it objectively and another to experience it in the heat of the match: you want to get to the ball, and your hand has a will of its own.

I always remember a ref who disallowed a goal I scored with my hand against Vélez, many years after Cebollitas, when I was playing for Argentinos, years before Mexico '86.

He warned me not to score that way again; I thanked him, but told him I couldn't make any promises. I can imagine him ecstatically celebrating our win against England. I don't know—I just imagine it.

When I played for Boca, I scored one goal like that against Rosario Central and no one even realized it, no one even asked. I knocked it in—bam!—up close, toward the near post. When I was playing for Napoli, I scored one against Udinese and another against Sampdoria. When I scored the one against Udinese, Zico said to me, right on the field, "You're cheating if you don't say you scored with your hand." I shook his hand and said, "Nice to meet you, Zico. My name's Diego Armando 'Cheating' Maradona."

I know I'm a bigger idol in Scotland than anywhere else because of that first goal. I mean, there's no love lost for the English there, so I'm like Carlos Gardel—even bigger there than in my old neighborhood. I know the Scots came up with a chant they sing in the stadium when they play against the English. Once I asked them to write it down for me on a piece of paper and I still have it. It goes like this:

> *You put your left hand in*
> *Your left hand out*
> *In out, in out*
> *You shake it all about*
> *You do the Maradona and you turn around*
> *He put the English out!*
> *Oh Diego Maradona*
> *Oh Diego Maradona*
> *Oh Diego Maradona*
> *He put the English out out out!*

I don't understand English, but there's something about me sticking it to them with my hand. And when they sing it, the Scots look happy.

For me, it was like stealing from a thief: it's no crime in my opinion.

At the press conference, I didn't know how to get out of my predicament. At first, I kept saying that I had headed it in. I don't know—I was scared that since I was still in the stadium, they might disallow the goal. What did I know? But in passing I said to someone, "It was Maradona's head and God's hand." I said that thinking about all the boys who had died in the Malvinas War—it really choked me up—and I thought that "God's hand" made me score that goal. Not that I was a God or my hand was God's hand: that it had been the hand of God, that God had also been thinking about all those boys slaughtered in the Malvinas, and he had made that goal happen.

That's what I feel today, thirty years later.

But at that point it just came out. I heard that just one newspaper published the quote, just one! *Crónica*, *Crónica* of all papers, the same paper that had been essential to me getting picked up by Boca in '81. I had told that paper that Boca was interested in me—something I just made up—before anyone at Boca had been in touch with me. Anyway, *Crónica* ran the quote, which went, "I swear on my life, I jumped when Shilton did, but I hit it with my head. But you can see the goalie's fist, which is what caused the confusion. But I swear it was a header, no doubt about it. There's even a bump on my forehead. I made that goal with Maradona's head but with God's hand."

Ha! They read that back to me now, and I start laughing.

What was I going to say at that point? Was I going to rat out Ali Bennaceur, the poor referee?

Thank goodness I didn't, because when I saw him again, many years later—I was already living here in Dubai and he invited me to his house in Tunisia—he seemed like a really nice guy. "I'd allow that goal all over again, Diego," he told me. "Because I didn't see it and neither did the assistant ref. Dotchev didn't see it and he was in a much better position than I was, so no one could have seen it . . . Not one of the hundred thousand people in the stadium saw it." Great guy, Bennaceur. He really warmed my heart. A modest man dressed in a gray tunic, he opened up his house to me. No resentment whatsoever. At the gym in my house, I have two framed pictures, one next to the other: the first shows me making that hand goal and the other shows me shaking Bennaceur's hand, before the match, when the captains come together. I asked him to sign the picture for me and everything.

All the sticklers come after me now about technology. Well, you know what? I am 100 percent behind technology in soccer, but back then technology was not used—and it's still not. And if there had been technology then, or even earlier, England wouldn't have won the '66 World Cup, because the goal they made was an embarrassment. It was a foot and a half from the goal line, but they were awarded the goal.

It's true that had there been technology, they wouldn't have allowed that goal of mine. And today I am totally on board with the need for technology. What's more, I'm going to lobby for technology at FIFA if I ever get the chance. We're already talking about the fact that everyone, everyone in sports, wants transparency; everyone wants to celebrate a goal after they've seen the replay; everyone wants to know whether the player hit the ball with his knee or touched it with his hand. That's the way they do things in American football, rugby, basketball. And soccer can't keep ignoring technology. So let's pitch in, and I really mean that. I'm going to vote in favor of using technology at FIFA. Call it whatever you want, Falcon's Eye, whatever—anything but Hand of God, since that might rub the English the wrong way and I want the FIFA to bring the whole world together.

The truth is that after that first goal, we had the guts to attack England, something we hadn't done before I scored that goal with my hand. We hadn't attacked them straight on. Sure, we'd attacked, but only one out of every two chances we got. It's true that after that goal everything changed, but it's also true that by then we were much better organized as a team.

I know there's a documentary where Peter Reid says he still has nightmares about that game and wakes up in a sweat. But whenever I see him—and I've seen him on more than one occasion—he talks about the second goal, not the first. He always brings up that second goal. On that ESPN program, he said that my second goal was "a work of art," and that it made him want to give me a standing ovation, that there was no possible way they could have stopped me. And when we spoke face-to-face, he said, "When I saw that wild stallion picking up speed, I couldn't take the heat and I just ran towards the middle of the field, alone. I surrendered."

If you watch the goal again—I've been forced to watch it millions of times—you'll see that what he says is true. It comes rushing back, and I can see it right now. There it is— there it is, when Reid just lets me go. What a moment.

LADIES AND GENTLEMEN, HERE YOU HAVE IT: THE GOAL

The play starts with Enrique's pass. Regardless of the joke, his pass was fundamental. What if he had overshot by five feet, huh? What would have happened then? I wouldn't have received the pass the way I received it, and I wouldn't have turned the way I turned to get rid of Beardsley and poor Reid. Right when I turned, I got rid of the two of them—start counting—but Hodge (a third) was nearby, and he wasn't marking anyone. You can see then how Reid watches me shoot past, and I'm off and running, crossing from the right side toward the goal, six feet from the center of the field. That's what he was talking about when he called me a "wild stallion." So then Butcher comes at me for the first time. I fake toward the sideline and then do an inside hook. The Englishman passes right by, turns, and then comes after me. And I can feel him behind, on my right, almost breathing down my neck.

And I saw Valdano and Burruchaga, who were waiting for a pass to the other side, on the left, but there was no way I'd pass it to them! No way! That ball was staying with me—it was mine, nobody else's.

That was when Fenwick came at me. And at this point I'd like to take my hat off to the English. Now, I'm not big on flattery, but if we had been playing against another team, I would never, ever have made that goal! Another team would have knocked me to the ground way earlier, but the English are noble people. Notice how noble Fenwick is. He pawed at me, it's true, but not at my face, just near my waist, as if he were rocking a baby. I didn't even feel him, with all the speed and power I had going on.

That's why I say if we had been playing another team, we might not be watching that goal today. Afterward, someone read to me that Fenwick said he was aware of the yellow card he had gotten in the first half; in the second half he had to decide whether to risk getting thrown out of the match if he fouled me. I think by the time he made up his mind the ball was already in the net. He also said that if he saw me again, he wouldn't shake my hand, but I bet he would. I bet he'd shake my hand and even embrace me.

Butcher did kick me—and you have no idea how much it hurt! He kicked me low, to see if he could sweep me off my feet and knock me over. But I was so pumped that once I got three toes on the ball to knock it in, I couldn't have cared less about Butcher's kick. I felt it more back in the locker room: when I looked at my ankle, I couldn't believe how screwed up it was!

As I've said a thousand times, what my brother, El Turco, had told me had gone to my head—and to my feet. It might not have been conscious, and I might not have remembered it at the time, but it was in there. I decided to approach the play the way El Turco had told me to. That's what I said back then. And turns out that five years earlier, in '81, at Wembley, during a tour of England, I made a similar play and finished by tapping the ball sideways when the goalie came at me. The ball went just wide of the post, and I had already started to celebrate . . .

El Turco called me on the phone to say, "Stupid! You never should have touched the ball . . . You should have faked to one side! The goalie had already dived." And I answered, "Son of a bitch! It looks easy on TV." But he answered right back, "No, Pelu, if you had faked to one side, you would have caught the ball on the outside and kicked it with your right foot—see what I mean?" The kid was just seven years old! Well, the fact is that this time I played it the way my brother wanted.

But the truth is that Shilton gave me a hand. His worst mistake, as you can see, was not blocking me at all. I didn't have to fake him out; I just had to push the ball forward. He did everything except block me the way a normal goalie would have. When I see it again, I can see how the goal took shape: I touched it and—plop!—a short kick, three toes to knock the ball in nice and soft. And that's it.

That time I really started screaming like a madman. I didn't even need to look at the referee. I knew what I had done. I ran along the end line, and when I reached the corner, I bumped into Salvatore Carmando, of all people. He embraced me and then the others ran over. Burruchaga, Batista, Valdano—they all forgot about Bilardo's warning about not getting nuts after a goal and wearing ourselves out. "What an amazing goal, you son of a bitch!" they shouted.

When I was with Bennaceur in Tunis, he also had something to say about that second goal. "You owe me for that goal, Diego," is what he said.

"Owe you? Why?"

"Because I could have stopped the play at the beginning, when the players said it was a foul. And then when you were off and running, I could have called foul two or three times, but you kept on going, and I was right behind you saying, 'Advantage! Advantage!'"

It's always the advantage rule. So the Tunisian also had something to do with that one. But, you know, he wasn't wrong about that. He understood the game. I was thrilled that he wasn't angry at me because, instead of remembering that as the worst mistake of his career, he just remembers that he was at that game. Got to love him.

In my view, that second goal is set to music. And the music is Víctor Hugo Morales's commentary. I've had to watch and hear that goal in English, Japanese, German. One day they even tricked me, showing me a video where the ball misses the goal at the end. But Víctor Hugo's commentary is like no other. That's why I am including it here, verbatim. Even reading it is like hearing it. And I get just as excited as the first time I heard it.

He's going to pass to Diego. Maradona's got the ball; he's got two men on, and Maradona kills the ball. The soccer genie takes off to the right, shoots past the third man and passes to Burruchaga! Always Maradona . . . Genius! Genius! Genius! Go, go, go, go, go . . . Goal!!! Goal!!! I want to cry! Lord almighty! Long live soccer! What a goal! Diego! Maradona! It brings tears to my eyes, forgive me! Maradona, in an unforgettable run, in the greatest play of all times, you cosmic kite, what planet did you come from? Leaving behind so many Englishmen, bringing the country together like a clenched fist, screaming for Argentina . . . Argentina two; England zero. Dieg-goal, Dieg-goal, Diego Armando Maradona! Thank you God for soccer, for Maradona, for these tears, for this . . . Argentina two, England zero.

That commentary and what my old man said later were a prize. A prize as great as the World Cup. My old man wasn't big on compliments; he would rarely say things like "I can't believe how you kicked that ball" or "what a great pass." But when we got together after that game against England, he hugged me and said, "Son, today you scored one hell of a goal." He told me he felt anxious watching the play, because he thought I would never make the shot, that I would fall or get knocked down. And that was when I realized I had done something truly epic.

It was so epic that we thought that it was over right then and there. But it wasn't, not at all. We were only ten minutes into the second half! We relaxed. We got overconfident, which is just what I had wanted us to avoid. I was always the sports-man, offering the other team water whenever they brought me water, even when the English started attacking us straight on, kicking balls that exploded like bombs. Nery saved one shot that Hoddle made on a free kick, and Hoddle was a great shot—I knew him well.

And I also knew Barnes—we all did. Tell me why Bilardo didn't send anyone to mark him! He left in "El Gringo" Gi-usti, who was worse at marking than I was, and he replaced Burruchaga with Tapia, because he was more skilled with the ball. But Barnes started causing trouble on the left, breaking past El Gringo over and over again. And the inevita-ble occurred: Barnes kicked it into the area, Nery stumbled, Lineker beat "El Cabezón" Ruggeri to the ball, and whenever Lineker got the ball, it went straight to the back of the net, and that's exactly what happened. Why put us through that? What need was there? Can you explain that to me?

That's when I realized I had to take the ball again, that we had to start over. And—check it out—I didn't wait one minute more: as soon as we kicked off from centerfield, I did a 360, just like the one I did for that second goal. I wanted to make the most of the fact that the English were all fired up and ready to attack. I looked for Tapia—there must have been some reason Bilardo put him in—and it turned out he was great for wall passes. And Tapia put so much passion into the shot he made that he pulled a muscle—but it hit the woodwork, the son of a bitch.

And then the English came back for another attack—always on the left side, because that's where they saw they had a chance, since Barnes could get around Giusti and Enrique, who had come downfield to help. But there was nothing to be done; we couldn't stop them. Right after that, there was a play a lot like their first goal. Check it out: Barnes broke away and passed to the area; the ball touched Enrique and went up straight over Pumpido. Then it came shooting down like a missile, toward the far post. And that was when God made his second play, the "nape of God." "El Vasco" Olarticoechea did a diving header into the goal, with Lineker practically lying on top of him. And El Vasco knocked it out of bounds—don't ask me how, but he did.

El Vasco saved us all, including Bilardo. What would people have said about the substitution Bilardo didn't make if that ball had gone in? What would people have said about Barnes shrugging off our defenders? Clausen should have come in there, man; he should have been on that field—anyone could have seen that.

Luckily, Bennaceur took mercy on us. He barely added any stoppage time. Check it out: he didn't even add a whole minute; the second period was over within forty-six minutes.

I went running over to the bench like a madman, and on the way, I ran into the guys I loved the most: Galíndez (Miguel Di Lorenzo), Tito Benrós, Roberto Molina (the team's masseuse), "El Ciego" Signorini. I shook Hoddle's hand. That went fine: no griping, nothing. But the field was a mess, photographers every-where, all of us embracing. Eduardo "El Tano" Forte, the jour-nalist from *El Gráfico*, asked me to kiss my jersey, and that's that picture that's on the cover of my book *Yo soy el Diego*. They couldn't have picked a better shot. That was the moment, my moment.

On the way to the locker room, one of the English guys—it turned out to be Hodge, but I wasn't sure at the time—asked me to swap jerseys with him. I said yes and we did. A few other English players came into the locker room to swap jerseys and someone sent them a few of mine. That's why I said, for us, the players, the war Falklands War barely a part of it.

At the drug-test station, things could have gotten tense, but nothing happened. Enrique, "El Tata" Brown, and I all went in singing, and there were the three English players. I remember Butcher, because he was the angriest, and because he was the one who had hacked my ankle during the second goal. Looking over at me, he tapped his head with his finger and then lifted his fist, as if to ask me whether I had scored the first goal with my hand.

"With my head, man. It was with my head," I answered, lifting my curls with my fingers. And it ended there. Still, I know that Butcher kept talking—he still does, in fact, as does Shilton. I think he's the only one. Because I've run into the other English players and they've always been gentlemen, never saying a word about it.

When we got back to the locker room and all the guys came over to congratulate me, Enrique said the phrase that would go down in history as much as my bit about "the hand of God." I can see him—his bulging eyes and white teeth—and hear him laughing as if it were today: "Hold on! Everyone's congratulating him but I'm the one who passed it to him. I served it to him on a platter!" Enrique was a star in every sense. A stellar player and a stellar human being.

Another thing I remember are all the kisses in the locker room after the game. Those were some seriously affectionate kisses. Right then, I felt like the greatest player in the world. The greatest by far. Valdano said to me, "Diego, after today there's no doubt in anyone's mind: you're not the best player in the World Cup; you're the best player in the world."

That was really something to say—you had to work for something like that. And after those two goals, it's true, I felt like I had finished off Platini, Zico, and Rummenigge for good.

While we were in the showers, I kept talking to Valdano and Burruchaga about the play. About how, when I attacked Reid, I saw two blue jerseys—their jerseys—off to the side. "One of them was Burruchaga's and the other was yours," I told Valdano. "But you were farther ahead and, unlike Burruchaga, asking for the ball. So what happened? You were the distraction."

Valdano turned off the faucet in his shower and then the one in mine, leaving me all covered with soap. He looked at me, irate, and said, "Stop! Just stop it!"

"What the hell's the matter with you?" I said. "What I'm saying is that you were the distraction and I want to thank you. If you hadn't gone in that direction, Fenwick wouldn't have been left wondering whether to head over to you or to stick with me to get to the ball even faster, you see? Fenwick antici-pated what you were going to do, and that's why I kept the ball right here, on my foot, to make him wonder whether I was going to pass it to you or keep going, which is what I did. That's why Fenwick couldn't stop me—can you see that, Jorge?"

And Jorge stopped playing the intellectual, the thinker, the serious man. "Fuck off!" he said. "I'm out of here. I'm done! No more humiliating me. There's no way you saw all that: it's not possible."

I swear to you that I saw him. And I swear that seeing it helped me, because otherwise—it's true—Fenwick would have come straight at me and fouled me outside the penalty area. And if he had come out, I would have passed to Valdano, and he would have come face-to-face with Shilton.

I scored some sweet goals in my time, like the one against the Colombian team Deportivo Pereira in an exhibition match against Argentinos. A goal that everyone talks about but few actually saw. I scored goals better than that one playing for Cebollitas too, but those were goals that only my old man and my old lady saw. None of them was as important as this one, of course. I had never dreamed of anything like this. I couldn't have dreamed it.

That goal became part of soccer history.

Guys like Messi, Tevez, and Riquelme can come in here now and score ten goals each. Better goals than that one. But we were playing against the English, after a war—after a war that was still fresh in everyone's mind, a war in which seventeen-year-old boys had gone out to fight in Flecha tennis shoes, shooting pellets at the English, who decided how many Argentine boys they would kill and how many they would let live . . . And there's nothing that can compare to that. Parents told their children about it, and those children will tell their children. Because thirty years have already gone by. Thirty years. And they keep on telling the story.

Of course, kids today are on PlayStation, which is of no interest to me at all. PlayStation might make you a little toy player, not a great player. But the truth is that there are still ten-year-old kids out there today with "Maradona" tattooed on them. And that kind of insanity can only be explained by one goal. Or maybe two.

My goals against the English.

Watching the game again for the first time after so many years, I think the sweetest moment was when the referee blew the whistle and it was all over. When Argentina ended up beating England two to one, when it was all over and it went down in history that I made both goals. When I watch it again now, I want to call Buenos Aires and hug everyone all over again when the game is over—just the way I did back then.

I don't remember when I first watched those goals with my daughters. I honestly don't. All I know is that Dalma and Gianinna—and Jana too, whom unfortunately I didn't recognize as my daughter until she was eighteen—take pride in their father, in the goals he scored and in his career, and that makes me very happy. As happy as when, watching those goals and others, they said to me, "Daddy, when are you going to play again like you do in the videos?"

I get asked about that goal Messi scored against Getafe CF, but . . . please! Come on! I scored a better goal than that against Deportivo Riestra, if you want to go there. Let's avoid stupid, idiotic comparisons, because they don't let Messi be, and they break my balls. "Because Messi scored a goal the same way—blah, blah, blah." Come on, don't screw with me—don't screw with us.

Messi may or may not be greater than I was. Now, I scored two goals against England, goals that honored the boys who fell in the Malvinas and their families. I gave them some consolation, and no one else—and I mean no one—is going to be able to do that. Because there's not going to be another war, because there can't be another war, because that would mean that a Galtieri was back in power—and no one wants another dictator.

It's impossible, totally impossible. It is possible that a more beautiful goal has been scored . . . but I doubt it.

What happened that day was unique. Beyond words. You can't write it; you can't say it. A lot of people say it combined the Argentines' talent and cunning. I don't know about that, but I do know one thing for sure, and I don't care who I offend when I say it. If I was just anyone, just some guy from Villa Fiorito, I would say, "Boy, I would have loved to score one hand goal and then another incredible goal against England." If I was just anyone, a kid from Villa Fiorito, I swear that's what I'd think.

CHAPTER 8

Maradona versus Maradona

ARGENTINA 2, BELGIUM 0
—*Mexico City, Wednesday, June 25*

No, please, don't. Don't compare the goal against England to the goals against Belgium. That is what I said to my brother, who was the first one to make the comparison, and I later said it to everyone else: don't tell me that that goal is better than the one I scored against the English. The goal against the Belgians was a nice goal, but it's a goal you could score in any match. You start off with strong legs, to shake off your marker, and then angle the ball toward the far post. I was so fast that diving wasn't even necessary—I was killing them with speed alone. So there are no secrets to that goal, to those goals. Or maybe there's one: at that point in the World Cup, when it came time for the semifinals, we felt invincible. And we didn't know at the time that we were playing against the best Belgian team in history. So that goal against the Belgians has nothing on those other goals. Nothing at all.

ON OUR WAY UP

They played a great game against us, I have to say. And you want to know something? They want to replay that match. Seriously, they called me not too long ago to say they'd like to celebrate the thirtieth anniversary with a friendly match. I would love to, because I thought they were a fantastic team and because I am really grateful for what their coach, Guy Thys, said at the time: "If Maradona had been playing for us, we would have won, two to zero." I was critical to that game: I outplayed myself, even though I didn't score a goal better than the one I had scored against England and I didn't play better than I had against Uruguay, which was undoubtedly my best match in that World Cup.

I was able to outplay myself because I had finally gotten across the idea that we were a force to be reckoned with. I told the guys, "We're going to really keep our head in the game, got it? These Belgians are no fools. There's a reason they made it to semifinals. We have to be strong right from the very start. As soon as we think we've won it, these guys will stick it to us, like they did against the Soviets."

The Belgians had gotten to that point playing it cool. When asked, they would say, "We've got nothing to lose." Well, yeah, the only game they had lost so far was their first game, against the Mexicans. And beating Iraq—I think it was—was no trouble, after which they tied against Paraguay, which had Romerito and Cabañas, who scored two goals against them. In the round of sixteen, they played the Soviet Union and won, four to three, though—if my memory doesn't fail me—the ref totally screwed the Soviets. Scifo scored a goal in that game, and in an interview he said that we were going to be the World Cup's biggest losers. Jan Ceulemans, a big guy who formed a great duo with Nico Claesen—another player I admired—played an amazing game.

Before they met up with us, they eliminated Spain, which had come from scoring five—five!—goals against Denmark, with Emilio Butragueño playing an amazing game. "El Buitre" Butragueño had this nice-boy face, the face of a kid who does all his homework, but he would rip you apart on the field. Nothing got past him, least of all Olsen when he messed up after an interception. He scored four out of five of those goals.

The truth is, rethinking that game, we should have been up against Spain, where José Camacho was a defender. How could I forget Camacho, who stomped all over me when I played for Barça? That's why now, with all the talk of marking and foul play, I would love to see the videos of those Barça-Madrid matches. My God, did those guys hack at us! There's a final in the Copa del Rey where one of them kicked me right in the ass. Just the same, that Spanish team coached by old Miguel Muñoz wanted to play the game, not just play dirty. And the one who came off looking great in Mexico was Calderé, whom I would remember a few years later, at the US World Cup.

It turned out that after a game against Northern Ireland in the '90 World Cup—a game Spain won, but it wasn't easy—Calderé tested positive for . . . ephedrine! They said he had been taking something for bronchitis, that he had gotten the runs just like Passarella, but some dope said that he had gotten high.

The difference between him and me is that, in his case, a doctor came out to take the heat. The Spanish soccer federation had to pay a fine and that was that: Calderé kept on playing as if nothing had happened. When I tested positive, everyone washed their hands of it, from Grondona all the way down to Dr. Ugalde.

Calderé was a starter in the match against the Belgians, which ended one to one in overtime, with Pfaff playing an amazing game. Ceulemans scored again, and so it ended in sudden death. Pfaff blocked one of the penalty kicks and the Belgians won. We had decided they wouldn't make it past the semis, but to make sure of that, we really had to concentrate, I mean really concentrate.

At the World Cup in Brazil, when Argentina beat Belgium to get past the famous hurdle of the quarterfinals (which we hadn't done in twenty-four years), a lot of guys asked me whether that match we played in '86 came to my mind. The truth is, it didn't. First of all, because we were in the semifinals. And, second, because I think the whole situation was different. In Brazil, Belgium played against the United States. Their midfielders were strong and aggressive. Witsel, a midfielder for the Belgian team, was strong and aggressive. Then they had Fellaini, Mertens, and Hazard—a player I admire. They had a fighting spirit and you could tell that they had really come together as a team. I saw how the whole team would respond to Wilmots, tuning into even his slightest move. You could tell they knew their game. They could have beaten Argentina, sure, if we hadn't woken up.

As for us, well, we were on our way up, for real.

Everything I already thought about Mascherano was confirmed when Argentina played against Belgium in Brazil. And to think that people used to laugh when I said the national team was "Mascherano plus ten." Please, Masche is brilliant. But there's no word for what Masche did that afternoon. I remember him—little though he was—facing up to Fellaini and Witsel. A colossal player in a small package.

If we kept doing everything right in the game against Belgium, if we didn't get distracted, we were a shoo-in for the finals. We started off on the top of our game, but we got distracted pretty quickly.

THE BEST BELGIAN TEAM IN HISTORY

When I watch this game again, I see it all so clearly. They put Renquin in as a sort of sweeper, and three guys in front of him: Gerets, Demol, and Vervoort. Grün was working with them and also upfield, where he would try to play with Vercauteren and Veyt, and then on up to Claesen and Ceulemans for them to score. I was still mad at Scifo for what he said about us being the biggest losers.

I think this was the first game where they didn't send anyone over to mark me. In the first five minutes, I got in a few passes, one rabona, and a few feints. And as soon as I could, I ruffled Pfaff's curls. He blocked a kick of mine toward the corner of the net, and Valdano knocked it in with his hand on the rebound.

I don't know if it was because we started out so strong, or what, but about ten minutes into the game, we got distracted. It was our very first game in Azteca stadium, and I didn't want it to be our last, no sir!

Back then, you didn't have cameras watching your every move. All the better, because there would have been quite a controversy over what happened on our way in, after we went down the ramp that's out back behind the goal. We had a meeting right there, because I felt like we were letting them trample all over us. We had let them get cocky, and for what? It didn't matter that they were the best Belgian team in history. I grabbed Ruggeri and said, "Cabezón, get rowdy back there because this isn't going our way!"

And in the second half, we came out like a whole different team, with a whole different attitude. When Ruggeri, Valdano, and I got riled up, everyone was scared shitless—even our guys, so you can imagine the others. But I had to run things; more than ever I had to be on top of what was going on. I had to come out and win it alone. But it was thanks to my teammates that I got to be the star.

And six minutes into the second half, I started winning it.

STRAIGHT TO THE PENALTY AREA

We were playing slightly downfield, and they weren't able to get the ball upfield, which gave us some maneuvering room. At one point, we started from way downfield, with Enrique bringing the ball up and passing it to Burruchaga, who was right of center. I motioned for him to pass, and ran into the penalty area. What he did was amazing, just amazing. I ran in on a diagonal like a figure eight, and as soon as two of their defenders closed in (now I see that it was Veyt and Demol) and Pfaff came running out in a craze, I smacked the ball sideways, with my left foot, high up. The secret to that goal was beating the two defenders to the ball. I saw Pfaff coming over to block me and I chipped it past him.

I had—or we had, more like—paved the way. After that, it was just a question of holding steady. Still, it wasn't easy. They had possession of the ball more than we did, but they were also limited to square passes. I was somewhat isolated, so I had to make the most of every chance I got, every ball that came my way. I was really proud of that rainbow kick against Scifo, who fouled me, but I went right on. Once again the ref—a Mexican guy, Márquez—stopped me when I was heading right for the goal. That bastard should have let us play on—the advantage rule. But our strategy was clear: go for it, go for it. When it was one-on-one, no one could stop me.

I made my way out of a foul play and left "El Vasco" Olarticoechea all alone. He liked running up the left side. And, two minutes later, on the right, I lobbed it right to where Enrique was running. At midfield, the Belgians had knocked me down something ugly when I was just starting a run, but that Mexican ref didn't call a foul. On the left, on the right, down the middle. Those were the best minutes of the game and El Vasco got another shot, which Pfaff blocked with his chest. We were close to scoring the second goal, really close . . .

And finally we did.

The Belgians walloped the ball from their downfield, straight against Cuciuffo's chest; Cuciuffo made it there before the forward he was supposed to mark. And then that daredevil Cuciuffo got all cocky because he had gotten the ball. His official position was stopper on the left, but he headed straight for Pfaff, with total control of the ball. He soared through midfield, passed the ball to me because I happened to be right there, and expected me to pass it back. A daredevil, right? And I went along with it. That's why I say that I won that game with the help of my teammates (after all, any distraction comes in handy).

Why did I use Cuciuffo? Because the defenders always thought I would pass it back to him, which I never did. I hooked it against Grün and moved in on a diagonal, from midfield left, but straight into the penalty area. Cuciuffo continued running to my left, opening up the field for me, with all the Belgians off to my right.

The secret to that goal was my leg strength. I was so fast with the ball, so fast, that when poor Gerets got close enough to block me, I had already made the kick. And, once again, Pfaff had come out too fast, his yellow sweatshirt letting me know right where he was.

In the first goal, I had smacked the ball with my left foot to the goalpost right of the goalie; here I did the opposite, but with the same foot: I kicked the ball full on and knocked it straight into the left side of the net.

There was something special about that goal, something that "El Zurdo" López spotted and tried to explain to me later at the training camp. He said that there were two reasons I might stick my tongue out during a game: first, because I liked the way it felt and, second, because it helped me keep my balance. And if you watch that goal, I'm always leaning left but I never fall, not even when I run off to celebrate with a closed fist in the air, because I knew I had kicked it at just the right moment. From then on, El Zurdo would always say, "Diego, don't forget to stick out your tongue, don't forget." But things like that didn't cross my mind, they just happened.

The thing that did cross my mind every time I scored—I am not sure why—was my mother, doña Tota, and how happy she must have been. And when I came back to midfield, after hugging Olarticoechea, who was the first one to make it over, I looked over into the stands where I knew my old man, don Diego, was sitting, and held up my closed fist.

I thought of them the way you think of the people who have always believed in you, not the fair-weather fans. And that was the moment. At that point, everyone was behind us, and I didn't like that one bit: it scared the shit out of me. With so many people against me, it would have been easy to relax, to let things be, to rest on my laurels. But we were not an easy group. We had really gotten used to having everyone against us, to it being us against the world. We needed that to enjoy things even more. And boy, did we enjoy things. We enjoyed winning like crazy.

HEROES

We had scored two goals against Belgium. I wanted to score a thousand! Not because of them, but because of all the others, those who had attacked us with no mercy.

Earlier that same day, Rummenigge's West Germany had taken Platini's France out of the cup and Zico's Brazil was already back in Copacabana. Just one game left to show them what I knew inside: I was the best. I had enough confidence to beat anyone: Platini or Rummenigge, who was quite a gentleman. But what mattered most was that there was only one game left for us to prove that we were the best and show how much we had grown as a team. If you saw how Batista and Burruchaga played the final match, oh Lord!

We were so relaxed by the end of that game that we gave "Bocha" Bochini the pleasure of playing. When there were five minutes left, he came in for Burruchaga, of all people. For me, that was something special: everyone knows he had been my idol when I was a boy. I loved the way he played. He was a pleasure to watch on the field. Even though he said he didn't feel like one of the champs, I think having played that match was like a trophy for him. I think he came to understand that later on. El Bocha is a little crazy, but he's going down in history as a great player. And we were all champions, each and every one of us, even the guys who never left the bench. Even Passarella, though he doesn't deserve to be. And that's why, when they made a movie out of that World Cup, they called it *Hero*. By this point in the cup, we had proven that that's just what we were: heroes.

I remember that in the middle of the cup the Italians at RAI decided to do one of those typical TV specials they were known for, mixing musicians with celebrities and soccer players. Right smack in the middle of the World Cup. And they asked me, Platini, and—I think—Rummenigge to each choose a guest singer. I think Platini chose a French woman— I don't remember her name—and I chose Valeria Lynch, who was really popular in Argentina then. They brought in Astor Piazzolla, the tango musician, too. When the Italians put something together, they do it big.

They were expecting me to be there too, even if no one had bothered to inform me; I mean, it would have been crazy to leave right in the middle of the cup. My mind was on the game and nothing else. When a car showed up at the training camp to pick me up, I said, no way, no one told me I was going any- where. But the Italians knew what to do. They did the program, Valeria sang, and later—with everyone's permission—they flew her to the training camp. I told her she was my idol, and she said the same for me.

Even today, I get chills down my spine every time I see the scene in the movie *Hero* where Valeria Lynch sings "Me Das Cada Día Más" ("Every Day You Give Me More") while I am doing warm-ups in slow motion. I wanted to give the Argen- tines a little more every day. And at that World Cup that's what I was doing. We weren't quite there yet—there was one last step.

CHAPTER 9

That's Right, World Champions

ARGENTINA 3, WEST GERMANY 2

—Mexico City, Sunday, June 29

When Claudia flew to Buenos Aires to give birth to Dalma, I really learned what it means to be nervous. But that night before the final against West Germany, I couldn't sleep at all. That had never happened to me before and it hasn't happened since: soccer never made me nervous. What did I have to be nervous about? I knew what I had to do out there. In soccer, things are easy: either you dribble your way past an opponent or he steals the ball from you. And, thirty years ago, I was convinced that none of my opponents would be able to steal the ball from me.

But just the same, I tossed and turned that night. I looked over at Pasculli, who was wide awake too. We went out for a walk and ran into Valdano, who was there in "the island"—as we called the other sleeping area—where only one guy was sleeping like a baby: Trobbiani. That lucky bastard—I have no idea how he possibly managed to get any sleep.

Valdano, who really had a way with words, said that stage fright was what was keeping us up. But I wasn't afraid. I wanted the match to start as soon as possible. And I didn't want to wear myself out waiting.

Or walking, for that matter. We had waited so long for that moment; we had fought so hard to get there . . . No, it wasn't fear of losing. It was fear that the game would never start. At least, that's how I experienced it. Plus, I have no idea why but the training camp was crammed with people on the day before the game: Saturday, June 28. Bilardo let every single Argentine who had come to Mexico on the premises.

MY OLD MAN KNEW

On Thursday, we had met with the press. Back then, there weren't any special rooms for press conferences, so when I saw the horde coming, with cameras and all, I went running out to the training field. A lot of them thought I was running away, but that wasn't it. When I reached the fence, which was just a little shorter than me—it came up to my neck—I took hold of it and jumped over. And then I invited the press to come over. I talked to every single one of them, but I was on the field and they were off it. I spent an hour talking to them. I was so happy. I couldn't stop laughing. I laughed my head off. And I didn't even get pissed when one of those chumps— there's always at least one—asked whether I had blown kisses into the stands to try to win over the Mexicans. What did I care about the Mexicans?!

"I'm no phony. I don't blow kisses into the stands to win people over—not the Mexicans or anybody else," I answered. "I respect the Mexicans like I respect everyone—let them cheer for whoever they want to. I blow kisses to my old man, who's always sitting up in a box seat. And let me tell you, if I blow a kiss, it's because I feel like it."

And my old man was one of the people who had said that he liked the West German team a lot. But he didn't say it then, when there were just three days to go before the final. He said it before the World Cup even started! My old man was wise, really wise. That's what was going through my head while we were waiting for the match to begin.

We were looking for distraction, any distraction. Take Friday, for example: with forty-eight hours to go, we had to do our pregame ritual of going to Perisur mall, just like we had done two days before all the games, starting with the first one. Early that evening, just past six o'clock, the same bus headed out of the training camp's gate. The same two guys, Tobías and Jesús, were on motorcycles out front, but there were also seven security cars taking up the rear. I swear I couldn't believe what I saw when the gate swung open: there were more people there than at Azteca stadium. I think that's when I realized exactly what we had achieved. I mean, at the beginning, there hadn't been such a fuss: we were a team no one believed in. And now we were in the finals, the World Cup finals! And we were on the bus—security guards and all—as if we were heading to the stadium.

It was a mob scene. "El Loco" Galíndez and I ended up trapped in the ice cream parlor we would always go to—Helen's was the name, I remember it well—after jogging our way through the mall. I was wearing Salvatore Bagni's Italian jersey, also for good luck. We were there for two hours. At about eight o'clock, we started back to the training camp. I think I signed more autographs at the mall than I had during my entire career at Napoli. Even our masseuse, Roberto Molina, was signing autographs. And then we holed up again, back in the little room I shared with Pedro, which felt like home at that point since we had decorated the place with pictures and newspaper clippings. After all, we had been there since May 5 and now, before we knew it, it was Sunday, June 29.

NO SUCH THING AS SECOND PLACE

I don't think I've ever been as happy to be up at seven-thirty in the morning. At that hour, I'm usually sleeping like a baby, but that day was different. I was imagining Tito Benrós putting together the team's apparel over at Azteca stadium. My Puma King cleats, which were always nice and shiny. I don't know how he did it, but he always left them looking brand new.

"What polish do you use, Benrós? Come on, tell me, that way when I get back to Napoli and you're not there, I can keep my cleats looking this good."

But he never said a word. Later I found the secret in a book he wrote: silicone cream mixed with kerosene, a rub they use on saddles, which makes perfect sense because I was quite the stallion back then.

We were all lined up in front of the bus half an hour before we were supposed to leave—just like we had been on the day we played England. We had to leave for Azteca stadium at nine thirty; by ten minutes to nine we were all dying to be on our way. It was already sweltering hot, and the game was at noon. Sons of bitches. Still, I think that ended up being harder on the West Germans than on us.

We sang soccer songs during the whole ride to the stadium. As usual, it was the troublemakers in the middle who started up—Islas, Almirón, Tapia, and me. When we arrived, we went right into the locker room as if we owned the place. We had already played there twice: first against England in the quarterfinals and then against Belgium in the semifinals. We already knew where Cuciuffo would put Our Lady of Luján, where each of us had to sit, and how Nery had to go spend some time out behind the goal where I had scored against England—the whole thing. Azteca stadium was like home to us, though we weren't going to have the warmest welcome that day. At the time, I said, "Pan-Americanism, my balls," because I couldn't believe that people in the stands were cheering for West Germany, a European superpower. It was one thing when they cheered for the Koreans, but for the West Germans? Whatever, it's ancient history now. Anyway, maybe it was good for us. After all, we didn't want to get cocky and believe that we were the best now that the fair-weather fans were behind us.

That's why I said what I said before we went out on the field. I spoke straight from the heart: "Boys, we've come far, but it's all for nothing if we don't win today. There's no such thing as second place. Let's think of everyone, guys. Our families, first, and our friends; the ones who stood behind us when no one else did and watched us suffer like dogs . . . Let's also think of all the folks who are just waiting for us to lose so they can do us in . . . Let's go—you hear me? Let's go get them, damn it!"

There were 115,000 people in Azteca stadium—115,000! And we had made it there without losing a match, in spite of all the doomsday predictions and the naysayers. Five wins, each better than the last, and just one tie. And we never even had to play extra time. In ninety minutes, we had beaten all of them, one after another. The Koreans, the Italians, the Bulgarians, the Uruguayans, the English, the Belgians . . . That was something: we were really making history out there, man. Italy, our classic European rival, out the door. Uruguay, our classic Río de la Plata rival, out the door. England, our classic rival in all senses, and with the Malvinas to boot, out the door. The only classic rival missing was Brazil. But it wasn't meant to be: the Brazilians had played a great game against the French team led by that heartless turkey Platini, but they ended up losing in the penalty shoot-out. Zico, who was supposedly going to compete with me for the crown, didn't do so well that World Cup: everyone could tell he wasn't at his best physically. Sócrates and Júnior both gave it their all, but it wasn't the same team Telê Santana had taken to the World Cup four years earlier.

And France had lost to West Germany in the semifinals, mostly because of Platini, who had to make some magic right then and there but didn't manage to shake his marker, Rolff. Plus, like I always say, you have to shoot a German ten times to bring him down, because Briegel pushes you from behind, Magath gets the ball at midfield, Matthäus moves it forward, and then either Brehme or Völler sends it into the back of the net, just like they did against the French.

And now the West Germans were up against us. These guys had plenty of experience. They had gotten to the finals in Spain '82; they had Beckenbauer on the bench—and Beckenbauer knew plenty about the finals. And there we were—a gang of rebels fired up by everything that had been said about us—ready to face them. Of the twenty-two Argentine players, only five of us had been at a World Cup before, and one of those five was Passarella, who was watching from the stands. The other four were Nery, "El Vasco" Olarticoechea, Valdano, and me. Of course, the four of us were starting.

For the fourth time since the match against England, we repeated the same lineup. So now, unlike in the first matches, you can really talk about a sweeper, about stoppers, about wingbacks. Everyone remembers the lineup from that final, so, of course, do I.

Nery was goalie; "El Tata" Brown was sweeper; José Luis Cuciuffo and "El Cabezón" Ruggeri were stoppers; "El Gringo" Giusti was right wingback and "El Vasco" left wingback; "Checho" Batista at midfield, a little farther back; Enrique as right midfielder; Burruchaga as left midfielder; Jorge as forward; and me, out there on the loose, wherever I wanted to play.

They had Schumacher tending goal. Brehme—who would score against us four years later when Codesal made up a penalty—was out there; Förster and Jakobs as center backs; the strongman Briegel as fullback; at midfield, Berthold, Matthäus, Eder, and Magath, who was supposed to control the ball; and Allofs and Rummenigge as forwards.

EVERYTHING AGAINST US

We walked up the ramp that went from the locker rooms to behind one of the goals as if we were heading home. I was at the front and Burru was at the back. That's the way we always went in. No exceptions. Before hitting the field, we repeated the show "El Tata" Brown and I had put together before playing Bulgaria, a match that felt like a century ago. The Germans are pretty serious people: they looked at us like we were crazy, but they didn't bat an eye. I said to El Tata, "Hard to get a rise out of these guys, huh?"

I had already had a serious talk with Brown in the locker room. "Tata, you're the best sweeper in the world, you got that? The best in the world . . . You may not start at Deportivo Español, but there's no one here like you, no one at all. You're going to rip these Germans' heads off—you got me?" And I kissed him on the top of his head. And then, screwing around, I asked, "Who's the son of a bitch that cuts your hair?"

When we stood at midfield for the national anthem, we got focused and serious. The national anthem got to me like it always does: it fills my heart, makes my chest swell. It makes me feel like my captain band is too tight on my arm, makes me tighten my grip on the pennant. And my whole life comes back to me, all of it. I think of Villa Fiorito, where I was born, and how far I've come. That's what I used to think about—and still do—whenever I hear the national anthem.

We were there to play the final under that giant spider that everyone probably remembers because it cast a shadow over us. It was some sort of television camera or who the hell knows . . . But it looked like a spider painted on the grass.

As soon as the anthem was finished, El Tata and I started yelling. We crouched down and leaned forward, and shouted, "Let's go get 'em, man. Let's do it!" We were like eleven madmen ready for war. If we were headed into hostile territory, all the better. And one minute into the game I realized it was going to be hostile territory. The ball was passed to me but it slipped away and went out of bounds, and the crowd started booing. So that's how it's going to be? Everyone against us? You'll see!

Or *almost* everyone, because there were Argentines there,

as well as Italians—or should I say Neapolitans. We suddenly had all these new fans from all over the place. Charter flights were bringing people in from Argentina—charter flights! Even government officials had come—that's right, the same ones I had stopped when they wanted to fire Bilardo.

Three minutes in, they fouled me for the first time, and I realized I was going to have Lothar Matthäus on my tail the whole match. His was no regular man marking. It wasn't Rolff, the guy they had sent to mark Platini. No, this guy knew how to play. Lothar was in amazing shape and he wasn't too big either. He was quick and he knew how to mark a guy. If he stole the ball from you, he would make a quick pass to one of his teammates. He could have been a playmaker or an attacking midfielder, but he ended up playing sweeper. Lothar was great out on the field—and a friend of mine as well. But that afternoon, he was my rival, my archenemy.

When I understood how they planned to play it, I led Matthäus over to the right side. If I didn't score, someone else would. I didn't care whether or not I scored; what I wanted was for the team to score. So I decided to lead my marker off to one side, thinking of the team, not about looking good personally. At the beginning, Matthäus—who, like I said, was a really clever player—wouldn't bother to follow me when I headed too far to either side. But Beckenbauer ran over and shouted at him to follow me wherever I went.

Watching the match now, for the first time in thirty years, I realize that despite all the blows I took, my memory is intact. The match is just as I remember it, minute by minute, though of course I want to fast-forward to the penalty kick that bastard Arppi Filho didn't call when I got fouled.

Arppi Filho, of all guys, the same ref who had officiated the game against Peru in June '85, when we qualified.

But let's take it step by step. Let's get to the game, which wasn't just any game. It was the World Cup final.

WE HAD TO HAVE THE BALL

Five minutes into the game, we let the Germans know that we were the ones making the rules. "El Vasco" Olarticoechea—what a phenomenal player he was—put pressure on the left and forced a corner kick. I delivered a great kick from the corner, but "Checho" Batista missed the opportunity. Schumacher, their goalie, wasn't following what was going on too closely. He was already messing up. It was time to attack. High balls, low balls: attack any way we could.

But we also had to defend, and you can see me lending a hand downfield. I really worked that whole game, no freeloading for me. If someone had to run to recover the ball, I was off and running. To make matters worse, they had put in Berthold, who played for Verona and would later play for Roma, to improve their game. Because with Matthäus marking me, they were one man down. But not us: we weren't missing anyone.

We did have this other separate game going on the field, though. It was Valdano versus Briegel, Briegel versus Valdano. Briegel was a bodybuilder who ran triathlons and God knows what else. His veins were like sausages and his calves were as wide as my chest. About fifteen minutes into the game, Briegel came at us like a tank. Jorge couldn't stop him, and Briegel dove just outside the penalty area. It was not a foul, no way! But the Brazilian ref called a foul. The Germans got a free kick, and since we had seen their two-touch kick against France, we went straight for them. Arppi said we had encroached and let them retake the kick. I complained, and the guy gave me a yellow card—a yellow card! Fifteen minutes in and the Brazilian ref had marked me worse than Matthäus had. On the second free kick, the ball rebounded off me. I had moved forward once again to block them.

The anger was back. You're all against us? Really? You'll see. I headed up the right side, where I had taken Lothar for a stroll and then back-heeled it to Cuciuffo. The Germans knocked him over and Matthäus stuck out his arm and smacked me in the face, so we got a free kick and the German got a yellow card. That's the way, Mr. Brazilian ref. You had no choice.

Burruchaga put an outward curl on his free kick from the right, and it curved away from the goalie. To make matters worse for them, Schumacher, who was already sweating bullets, went anywhere except where he should have gone. And the ball went sailing straight for one player's head . . . but whose? One of the big guys who was always right there: that's right, but was it Ruggeri or Valdano? Or maybe "El Tata" Brown? No sir! The ball came straight toward my head. Brown's goal should have been mine; it was mine. Check it out—watch the play. But El Tata knocked me over—he fouled me! He leaned on me and knocked me over, and then smacked the ball with his forehead. Good for him. He deserved it more than I did—more than anyone! He didn't even play for any club, but he was an ace. And, hey, if the ball had come to me, I might have just grazed it and knocked it out of bounds, who knows?

Anyway, it was twenty minutes in and we were winning,

one to nothing. And they were down a player, because Matthäus wasn't exactly playing. And we were up a player because Burruchaga is the man. My lieutenant, the guy who had to get to the ball when I couldn't. And that's just what Jorge did. Like all of us, he had grown as a player as the World Cup progressed. And by that seventh match he was really something.

The Germans start bombarding our defense with centers. But "El Cabezón" Ruggeri was downfield to knock every one of them out, and the Germans were constantly getting called offside.

Twenty-five minutes or so into the first half, I took a free kick. Watching it again now, I should have kicked it differently. I should have stood closer to the ball and chipped it higher, to get it over the wall, instead of kicking toward Schumacher's goalpost, which is what I did, and he saved it. That is one of the reasons I say I played better in '90 than in '86. Four more years of experience, four more years of kicking...

At that point in the game, we started carving out new spaces for ourselves on the field. Even "Checho" Batista made it into the box. He wasn't an ace when it came to kicking, it's true, but he did make it all the way up there. I got ahold of one of the balls they cleared from inside the penalty area just outside the semicircle and I started a run, the way I liked to do at that World Cup. I got past one German and then another, but the third German knocked me down. I think it was Jakobs. And the ref, Arppi, not only didn't give him a yellow card, which he deserved, but also stepped on me when he ran over.

Thirty minutes in and we had a few more almost-goals. In

one of them, I shot a double-wall pass to "El Gringo" Giusti, who back-heeled the ball to me—yeah, "El Gringo" Giusti back-heeled it! Schumacher came sliding out feetfirst, and the ball rebounded off me and almost went in.

That's how the first half ended. They had had a few shots on goal, that's it. We had to keep control of the ball. The ball had to be ours. Still, they couldn't get within range. Cuciuffo was all over Allofs, forcing Beckenbauer to send in a sub. And Rummenigge spent the whole game complaining that Nery was holding too long. When I see that back-pass to the goalie today, I can't believe that used to be allowed.

We didn't have to change our strategy for the second half, but we did have to stay alert. In their first free kick that half, something that had been working well came out horribly: "El Gringo" Giusti messed up the offside trap and "El Tata" Brown had to give it his all to beat Völler, who had subbed in for Allofs. And that's exactly what El Tata did: his shoulder was hurt badly, and after that play, he couldn't straighten his arm. All our jerseys were made of eyelet, so they had tiny holes in them, which was great, but the jersey El Tata was wearing had a big hole so he could stick his thumb into it and keep his arm half bent. That's how he played the second half. A real trooper.

We kept at it, despite so many difficulties. We made it into the area again, this time with Burruchaga, and that's when we scored the second time. That goal really shows how Valdano played: he started off like a center back because that's where he was positioned, marking a German player on one of their free kicks, but then he dashed off on a diagonal. Along the way, I happened to get the ball because a German slide-tackled Jorge and tapped the ball away from him. It looked as if Valdano was the one who passed to me, but it was actually that German guy. I passed left, aiming for Enrique, who was always where he was supposed to be. In the meantime, Valdano kept on running on a diagonal, crossing the entire field from end to end. Enrique dribbled a few feet and then made a pass that was destined to end in a goal: the ball went straight to Jorge's feet, perfectly positioned for a fast break, with no one in the zone. Valdano bolted toward the goal and, once again, Schumacher was at a loss. It took the goalie too long to come out to block, and Valdano leaned left so that the ball was on his right foot. He lifted his foot and—plop!—drove the ball into the right side of the net. What a goal. Ten minutes into the second half and we were winning, two to nothing.

Was the game over? Not by a long shot!

IT SHOULD HAVE BEEN A PENALTY

From that point on, the Germans bombed us with centers, one high ball after another. And Beckenbauer took out Magath, who hadn't touched the ball, and put in a giant named Hoeneß. Clear as a bell. That's why we had to have possession of the ball and keep trying to score. At one point, Valdano almost headed it in, but the ball went just wide of goal. Later on, Berny Ulloa—the same line ref who made me pick up the corner flag in the game against the English—made a terrible offside call against Enrique.

When there were twenty minutes left in the game, I met up with Valdano on the right; Matthäus could no longer keep up with me. Valdano, Enrique, Burruchaga, and I were putting together a sweet play when the Germans stole the ball.

We were on our way, ahead two to nothing, when suddenly the tides turned. On that fateful corner kick, two of us
were glued to the goal, one on each post, freeing the Germans
up to do whatever they wanted; Rummenigge got the ball in
after it grazed the head of one of our guys—I'm not sure whose
head it was and I don't want to know. And then, right away,
another corner, with all of us glued to the box, two headers
and the second one—the one off of Völler's head—went in . . .
two to two. Two headers inside the penalty area, goal.

The thing my old man had said about German blood came
to mind right then: you have to knock them down over and
over again if you want to beat them. But you want to know
the truth? When they tied it up, it never even crossed my
mind that we might lose the game. I had been asking for the
ball, but now I started demanding it. We had to come up with
something: there were eleven of them, but it had to seem
like there were twenty-two of us. And that's what we did. The
team came together even more when, after it had seemed
like we had it in the bag, they tied it up.

When we kicked off after that second goal, I slammed the
ball down in the center circle and yelled to Burruchaga,
"Come on, they're beat. They're done running! Let's get it
moving. Let's show them how we play the game and win this
with no extra time!"

Three minutes later, in a game that could have meant the
end of everything we had been working for—three minutes—
leaving seven minutes to go before the ninety-minute mark,
and, first I had a free kick that ran into the wall. Then right
away Enrique—again—beat a German to the ball and flicked
it to me. The ball bounced up and came down right in front of
me. None of the Germans dashed for the ball; they were

wiped out. I saw a blue-and-white jersey run past and—plop!—
I passed it on upfield. No one had yelled or called for the ball.
No one. The guy in that blue-and-white jersey happened to
be Burruchaga, and I got the ball to him quickly. When I saw
Burru start running, I looked the other way and spotted a
guy in a green jersey up ahead, which meant that no one
would be offside. It was Briegel, who was on his last legs.

So off went Burru, straight for the goal. Once again Schumacher was at a loss; he never even came out, and Burru
drove it on home. Boy, did I yell when that goal went in! If I
hadn't lost faith when they tied it up, imagine how I felt now.
I already felt like we were the champions of the world, but Bilardo started shouting at us to mark them, mark them . . . But
it was over, I knew it was over.

I ran into Schumacher at the anti-doping station and we
talked. He was fluent in Italian.

"Good thing you won it three to two, because if it had
gone into overtime, you would have scored five. We couldn't
go on playing. Our defenders were shot," he said.

I do remember how their faces were flushed from ex-
haustion. We ran straight to the end, but that's because mentally we were really strong. I mean really strong. Check out
the penalty play—the penalty shot Arppi Filho didn't call because he's a cocksucker. I was running circles around them.
Valdano, Burruchaga, and I put together a great play: I went
right past the Germans; one of them fouled me, but I recovered the ball and headed straight for Schumacher. Right then
Jakobs was moving in as well. I tapped the ball and Schumacher plowed right into me. Man, that was a penalty, hands-
down. There were three minutes left, and they didn't call
that penalty. But no sweat—I didn't even care.

"It's over, Arppi, it's done. Blow the whistle and quit screwing around," I called out to the Brazilian ref. There was still time for "El Tata" Brown to beat out Rummenigge one last time, to prove—like I had said in the locker room—that he was the world's best sweeper. There was still time for Trobbiani to come in and make a spectacular back-heel: they had knocked me against the flag that's placed at midfield in another foul. I could have stayed on the ground for a while, but I got right back up and smacked the ball over to Trobbiani, who stopped it and, as if he were playing in his own backyard, back-heeled it to Enrique, who took off to face Schumacher alone. But the German finally stopped one. Imagine how great that would have been for Enrique, scoring a goal in the final . . .

And then the Brazilian ref—it had to be a Brazilian—finally ended it. And so we were the champions of the world. Do you know what that means—to be a champion of the world wearing your country's jersey? There's nothing like it.

UNDEFEATED

I said it then and I'll say it again now, thirty years later: that was the peak of my career. Nothing else compares. Because of the way we won it, man. We didn't lose a single game—no one was able to beat us—and we scored, like, fourteen goals. It wasn't just the championship I had dreamed of; it was the one all Argentines had dreamed of. Hats off to the Argentines who played in '78, because if it hadn't been for "El Flaco" Menotti and that title, we wouldn't have been anything but hopefuls with an empty trophy case. But the championship we fought hardest for, the one we most deserved, the most heartfelt and outstanding championship of all, was Mexico '86.

When I talk about that World Cup, my face lights up, and that's how it's going to be until the day I die.

When the whistle blew, I dropped to my knees. People were embracing me—I don't even know who they were, because the fans stormed the field right away. And naturally I gave Bilardo a hug—how could I not? I see it again now and I can't believe he forgot about all that, forgot how hard we worked. I called the journalists fair-weather friends, and I asked them to apologize to Bilardo and the whole team. Whenever my teammates and I talk about the World Cup, we say how important it was that we left Barranquilla for Mexico. That decision—a decision entirely our own—took us halfway to the championship. It allowed us to get used to the altitude; as the days passed, we built up endurance during practice, and if we could do it at practice, we knew we'd have even more endurance at the games. We spent two whole months—May and June—building endurance.

I put up with all the crap I had to put up with during those two months because I needed to win. I wanted that cup for my country—and for my teammates and for me. Because everyone had been against us and we wanted to prove to them what we were capable of achieving.

When I went up onto the platform to take the cup, Havelange didn't hand it to me. While I was walking up, he handed it to the Mexican president, and then the president handed it to me. I didn't care who gave it to me: the important thing was getting it. I held it in my hands the way you hold a baby. First I lifted it up and then I hugged it to my chest. Just like you would a baby.

The first one to come up was Nery, and I passed it to him.

Storani, the government official the Argentines had sent, touched my shoulder; maybe he wanted to say something to me, I don't know, because I didn't pay any attention. They hadn't supported us—they had no right to be celebrating with us. Nery passed it to El Tata, and then it went on to every last player. The only thing we wanted was to get down off that platform and do our victory lap.

As soon as I got down onto the grass, this guy came over and hoisted me up on his shoulders. I met up with him again not too long ago, since during the Brazilian World Cup he appeared as a guest on my TV program, *De Zurda*. I remember the guy begged me to give him my cleats: no way was I giving them to him! But the funny thing was that I was on his shoulders, guiding him the way you would a horse—come this way, go that way, spurring him with my legs. His name was Roberto Cejas and he had traveled to Mexico for the final. He told me that he had made the trip with seven friends, but they only managed to get four tickets to the game. But, being Argentines and all, they all managed to get into the stadium somehow. They spent the whole game behind the goal where El Tata scored the first goal, but when the match ended, they made their way over to a corner to climb down onto the field. This guy, like all the others who had invaded the field, waited for us to get the cup. When I first came back onto the field with the cup in hand, I thought they were going to trample me.

So I came face-to-face with this big guy and motioned for him to lift me up. He stuck his head between my legs and hoisted me up. I sure messed up his hair! So suddenly I had a bird's-eye view. It was quite a sight, let me tell you!

First I spotted Pedro Pasculli, my roommate, the guy I had spent more time with than anyone else; I got this guy to carry me over to where Pedro was. That's one of my favorite pictures.

It's an odd feeling: I didn't ever want to leave—I didn't want the happiness to end—but at the same time, I wanted to go back home, to be in my country, Argentina, to celebrate the victory with everyone. That was all I wanted.

I wouldn't let go of the cup. I carried it like a baby all the way to the training camp. Once we were back, I lent it to Grondona for a little while because he asked to hold it. When I got it back—don't ask me why—it didn't feel like the same cup. It was not as heavy. When they first handed me the cup in the stadium, it felt so heavy that it was hard to hold up with just one hand. My hand shook a little bit—that's how heavy it was. I looked at it and couldn't believe my eyes. I kept touching it to make sure it wasn't all a dream.

THROW THEM OUT AND NEVER LET THEM BACK

We got back to the training camp quickly. So quickly that we forgot all about Bilardo. None of us had packed our bags or anything—that would have been bad luck. And we had to leave for Buenos Aires that same day. But we made time to do something we had all promised one another: we took the victory lap around the field where we had trained. Just us, the team members, all by ourselves. We had gotten to Mexico on May 5 and it was now June 29. We deserved our own private celebration. That was the greatest victory lap of my career. Afterward, we downed all the alcohol we hadn't been able to drink for the past two months. I had promised Ricardo "El Profe" Echevarría that if we won the championship, we would drink a bottle of Chivas Regal. And we made good on that promise, boy. Bilardo, Madero, Pasculli, and Tito Benrós all joined in the fun. We drank it in my room, the room I shared with Pedro.

And—unbelievable but true—our plane left for Buenos Aires at 11:00 p.m. that same night. I still remember the captain's voice on the loudspeaker saying, "We are so proud to have the World Cup champions on our flight tonight." The World Cup champions! That was us. We flew coach on a regular Aerolíneas Argentinas flight; team management flew first class. We players were stuck in the back. El Cabezón and I took the last row, and once again it was all the whisky you could drink. We couldn't stop chanting and jumping up and down. We started off with "This one is for you / all you / motherfuckers."

Then we strolled up into the first-class cabin, where that government guy from the Radical party, Storani, was seated, and sang the march of his rivals, the Peronists. And then we switched to a special chant for all the suits: "These grumpy old men / refuse to shout. / These grumpy old men / refuse to shout. / Throw them out. Throw them out. / And never let them come back."

And they laughed it off like a joke. Today, that chant's worth millions of dollars.

At some point, I fell asleep—medal hanging around my neck and the cup in my arms. I think I had been awake for more than twenty-four hours straight, what with the anxiety the night before the game, the game itself, and the trip home.

When I woke up, we were landing at Ezeiza. And from there we went straight to Plaza de Mayo, to celebrate with the people, the way real champions do.

UP ON THE BALCONY, I FELT LIKE JUAN DOMINGO PERÓN

When I walked out onto the balcony of the Casa Rosada, the president's office, cup in hand, I felt like Juan Domingo Perón when he would go out there to talk to the masses. I've been a Peronist my whole life and I'll die a Peronist, because of my mother and because of Evita. In our sexist society, everyone talks about Perón, but Evita was a great woman. Women, like former president Cristina Kirchner, do great things. That's why I support her.

I love Peronism, and if I decide to go into politics one day, that'll be my party. I know what I want and I know what I don't want: for example, I don't support the new Argentine president, Mauricio Macri. I'm not talking about his performance as the president of the Boca club—he did fine there—but a country isn't a soccer club. We Argentines make mistakes, and we're so used to hard times that we can make a mistake in an election and bounce right back from it. We've been hit so hard that we don't even know which way to run. But as long as Macri is president, I'm not moving back to Argentina. That's why I say, know when to fight and know when to lay low. I won't give up, because I love my country. After 2010, I considered myself a sports exile, and today I consider myself a political exile. But, like I said, you have to know when to fight and when to lay low—that was true thirty years ago and it's true today.

And it's important to recognize that President Alfonsín did the right thing thirty years ago, after almost screwing things up royally with Bilardo, because he left us the balcony. He didn't insist on being out there with us; he took the back-seat. They say I didn't shake his hand, but that's not true. Before going out onto the balcony, when Alfonsín greeted us in one of the rooms, he embraced me, and I didn't pull away. One thing, though: I kept the cup in my arms. But I did let him embrace me because I thought it was a sincere gesture from a man who was truly grateful. Alfonsín knew better than anyone that we had made the people happy. And if the people were happy, I was happy. Because it wasn't his celebration and it wasn't our celebration: it was the people's celebration—the celebration of all the folks who had filled the square below, the ones who had so much hope. We had made them happy. I thought of them and I thought of my family. No one else.

When I remember it now, it's the same as it was back then. That feeling hasn't changed, not one bit: if it had been up to me, I would have gone down into the square with a flag and gone running into the crowds to celebrate. But when I left the Casa Rosada, I went home to the same house in Villa Devoto where my folks lived and died. A crowd had gathered outside the house—more people than had been at the square! And they stayed for days and days, and even spent nights there. I couldn't believe it. One time, I asked two little kids in, because I felt sorry for them. I couldn't do much more than that: if they all came in, they would have torn the house down. But letting those two boys in was symbolic, like letting them all in.

As I've said before, I felt something else, something besides that immense joy. I also felt a little sad. Because it seemed like too much, a bit over the top. As I've said, all I won was a World Cup, nothing more than that.

Now that thirty years have gone by and Argentina hasn't won the cup again, I realize what it meant—and what it still means—to the Argentines.

CHAPTER 10

The Next Champion

I've got the Argentine jersey tattooed on my skin, with the number 10 on my back and the captain's band on my left arm. Just because you can't see it doesn't mean I don't feel it. That's why it hurts that thirty years have gone by and we still haven't won the cup again. It hurts me deep in my soul. I would have loved for the national team to win another World Cup, with or without me.

Why would I celebrate the fact that I never took another victory lap with that jersey on? How could that cross anyone's mind?

One guy actually wrote to me before the World Cup in South Africa, in 2010, saying that I didn't want the national team—my national team!—to win the World Cup because I didn't want to see Messi taking the victory lap, didn't want Lio Messi to outshine me. What an asshole. If we had won in South Africa, I would have another cup under my belt, only this time as coach! So to outshine me—if that's what this jerk thought I was afraid of—Messi was going to have to become a coach and then lead the national team on to victory in the World Cup. So, come on. It's ridiculous to think I didn't want us to win the championship in 2010. I've got only one thing to say to the guy who wrote that: He'll never know what it means to defend the national jersey. He'll never bolt down the field or even sit on the bench, biting the bullet.

TALENT CAN'T BE DISGRACED

Just for the record: I would love for there to be seven little stars atop the crest on our jersey today, in 2016. But no, damn it, we've only got two. And that's like a dagger in my heart.

There's an explanation for this, of course—you can explain anything, but that doesn't stop the pain. I could start by saying that if you show the Germans any weakness, they fire it into the back of the net. We've run into them on the field three or four times over the past thirty years, and they've always kept us from bringing the cup back home. To compare the 1986 and the 2014 teams, I would say that '86 team had more conviction, that we were at the top of our game in the final, that we got better and better with each match, and that even though the Germans might have scared us a bit, by the final we knew we were unbeatable.

In Brazil in 2014, Argentina looked tired from the first game to the last. I think there were maybe four or five players—no more—who performed well enough to say that they truly represented Argentine soccer. I won't name names, but Messi and Mascherano were two players who really gave it their all. But most of the guys just looked tired out there. Their playing style was humdrum. Without Messi's attacks, fans wouldn't even have stood up. And, in the final, a final where Germany didn't have the power to score—because they didn't—Argentina leaned on Lio too much, and he didn't play his best game. Argentina could have won, just the same. We could have made it. But we showed those Germans a little weakness and Götze drove it into the back of the net.

I agreed with Mascherano when he said he was sick of eating shit, and I think you could say that about these thirty years without another championship. I am sick of eating shit too.

The Brazil World Cup was really special for me. I co-hosted a television program with Víctor Hugo Morales, *De Zurda,* and loved every minute of it. Every night I invited a special guest in to talk. Of course, FIFA doesn't like people saying anything against it—and neither does the Asociación del Fútbol Argentino. They insulted me in the worst way ever by saying I was jinxing the games. Grondona and his guys called me a jinx, and I wrote them a letter to let them and everyone else know how I felt about that. And also to let them know that I had no intention of letting up.

The day I played my testimonial match, I said you couldn't disgrace the ball. I still believe that. After all, even though I stopped playing professionally, I am still a soccer player. The boys who go out on the field to play for Argentina's national team aren't eleven strangers to me: on the contrary, they're my friends, my brothers. Everyone who knows me knows I would never wish the team anything but success—I swear it on my country, my family, and my friends,

You'd have to be pretty screwed up to say that. I have given my life for the Argentine team, and I will continue to give my life for the team, on and off the field. Swollen ankles, ingrown toenails, tears of joy and of sadness for the sport: these are the trophies I carry.

And just as talent cannot be disgraced, the magic of a guy like Lionel Messi is unquestionable—and that's got nothing to do with jinxes or luck. Because if you want to talk about luck, I've been pretty damn lucky. I feel people's affection every day. The same people who loved me as a player continue to love me today: I see it in every picture, at every stadium where people chant my name, every fan letter that comes to *De Zurda,* and every embrace I receive across the planet.

We're building a whole new Latin America, one that defies the powers that rule the world. They can't wipe the smiles off our faces or take away the joy of celebrating a glorious World Cup. The fact that Latin Americans do so well at the World Cup is no coincidence.

The ball can't be disgraced, though some people would love to rip it into little pieces.

Although I beat the Germans on the field, I've lost to them over the course of these thirty years. First as a player and then as a coach.

IN ITALY, GRONDONA GAVE THE WORLD CUP AWAY

When I got to Italy in '90, I was in better shape than I had been in Mexico in '86. Soccer-wise too. I was twenty-nine. I had won the last ten games for Napoli single-handedly. Now, when I arrived in Mexico, I had some great games with Napoli under my belt, but by the time I got to Italy four years later I had two championships as well. Two championships with Napoli! I was still working with Dal Monte, with Signorini, and I could fly even higher than I had four years before. I remember we had

a treadmill there in Trigoria, and when I got off it, it was literally smoking. God, was I in unbelievable shape!

But even though I was at the top of my game when we started the '90 World Cup, we were dead by the time we got to the end. I had a torn muscle. Yup, I played the final with a torn muscle, something I've never admitted until now. Not to mention the ingrown nail on my big toe and an ankle swollen up like a ball. And the extra weight of having eliminated the Italians, of course. The stadium went from seeming like heaven to seeming like hell the moment that game ended. More than half the team was in poor shape, and we would be playing without Caniggia, who had done something stupid that ended up getting him another yellow card in the semifinal against Italy. And, on top of it all, Grondona gave the cup away. He actually said it to me in the shower, man, and I'm going to keep telling the story. No one told me this—I lived it.

The day before the match, we went to visit Olímpico stadium. We were in the showers, and Grondona came over. "It's over, Diego. We made it to the final."

"What? What the hell are you talking about, Julio?"

"It's over—we did all we could. Look how far we've come. Plus, you've got a torn muscle . . . It's over."

"What's wrong with you, Julio? Don't you want to win this?"

"Of course I want to win it, but having made it this far is quite an achievement, right? We're done, Diego."

I couldn't believe my ears. Done, my ass! We were playing the final match the next day and we were going to play to win. Had the match been fixed?

That's exactly what was said, word for word. I swear on doña Tota and don Diego. And I swear that I had a torn hamstring when we played Germany. They couldn't even do infiltration anesthesia, not with a torn muscle.

Bilardo said to me, "I'll put you in the second half."

"You wait until the second half to put me in and I'll kick the shit out of you."

I think we had ruined their business plans, and I mean big business! They had already made the flags—half Italian and half German—for the final match everyone wanted. But we left them *fuori* of the cup and made them lose *milliardi*, for sure. We knocked them out of a final that Matarrese had already fixed.

Even though we were all torn up, that German team wasn't any better than we were. True, they had Matthäus, who was a much better player than he had been four years earlier and who was no longer there just to mark me, the way he had been in Mexico. He ran the team.

Even though we were in such bad shape, they still had to rob us if they wanted to win. Let's be clear: the penalty they called wasn't even a foul. It wouldn't have been a foul if it had happened at midfield. But Codesal called a penalty, and later on he got named head referee in Mexico. How about that, huh? As the years go by, you start to see how the favor-for-favor thing works. And because Codesal went ahead and clinched the championship for Germany back then, here he is today with that same job. These are the things I want to see changed at FIFA. Never again.

By the '90 World Cup, my daughter Dalma could understand a lot of what was going on. A lot. She spoke perfect

Italian. But I felt the same way I did in Mexico in '86—I didn't want anyone or anything to distract me from my objective, which is why even though my family was in Italy, they didn't go to the matches. They would watch the games on TV with Claudia. They would put on the Argentine jerseys, which came down to their knees like nightgowns, and sit right in front of the television. Whenever I appeared on screen, Dalma would yell, "Diego! Diego!" That was the only time she called me Diego and not Dad. Dalma is usually the calm one, but she wasn't too calm when I came home after losing the final against Germany.

I had promised her the World Cup, so when I handed little Dalma the silver medal, she threw it at me. I swear I cried more then than I had at the stadium. How could I explain to her what it felt like to have been robbed? What for? I didn't celebrate that silver medal, not ever. I didn't want to shake Havelange's hand either. Even today I remember how bad I felt about not being able to bring the cup home to my daughter. I can't forgive myself for having failed her.

WHY WE HAVEN'T BEEN CHAMPIONS SINCE

When I coached the Argentine team, we also lost to the Germans. In 2010, Otamendi lost his footing and slipped, and Müller headed it in, a move we had been prepared for. We had decided there were four Germans who had to be marked: Khedira, Klose, Mertesacker, and Müller. And Müller would always position himself at the near post. As soon as we hit the field, Otamendi slipped and Müller drove it in, and so we started out losing, one to nothing. And we couldn't turn the game around.

If I had the match to play over again, I'd use the same strategy and play with the same team. Some people said I should have put in another midfielder, but which of the forwards could I have taken out? If I had taken out a forward, the German defenders would have been all over us. I'll argue this with any coach. A lot of people criticized me because I put in "El Gringo" Heinze and Otamendi as fullbacks. If I had had Roberto Carlos and Dani Alves like the Brazilians, I would have put them in, but I didn't have them (there were no Argentine defenders of their caliber). Now, let me say that I blame myself that we lost, four to nothing. But I can't blame Otamendi or "El Gringo" Heinze. On Monday morning, of course, the newspaper ran something about Maradona's inglorious stint as the coach of the national team. In my opinion, we had done great.

And they also said that in South Africa in 2010 Messi hadn't been for me what I had been for Bilardo in Mexico in '86. You want to know something? I'm the first one to say that's bull.

I think Messi had an excellent World Cup that year. He made every goalie who came up against him look like a star player, and he also made them millionaires! Every one of those guys was sold after playing the game of their lives and looking good up against Lio. So please don't tell me that Messi didn't play well at that World Cup. The last guy responsible for our defeat that year was Lio Messi. In my opinion, he was the best player on the national team.

And he would be the best again, in another World Cup. But I'll get back to him in a minute. Before that, I want to keep explaining why we haven't been champions in all these years, to talk about what has been going wrong.

THE DAMN EPHEDRINE

In the United States in '94, if we had continued playing the way we had been playing and I had been there for the whole cup, we would have been champions—no doubt about it. Because we had figured things out with "El Coco" Basile on the attack—what a tremendous player—though on the counter-attack, things could get iffy because of the players we had on defense. If you hear Simeone, Redondo, Maradona, Balbo, Caniggia, Batistuta, the first thing you ask is, "And who the hell was defending?" And the answer is, we always had the ball. We had an amazing team.

It's true that I felt like they had it in for me at that World Cup. I started suspecting that after I accused the team management of drinking champagne and eating caviar while we were out there killing ourselves on the field. Ever since I said that the first time, I felt like they had it in for me. But I keep saying the same thing I did back then: the truth, the real truth, of World Cup '94 was that Daniel Cerrini made a mistake but I took the heat. That's the one and only truth. No one had promised me anything. Some people said that FIFA had given me a blank check to do whatever I wanted and then they tricked me with the anti-doping test. That's a huge lie!

The only thing I asked Grondona afterward was for them to take into account that I hadn't done it to gain any advantage and so they should let me play, let me finish my last World Cup. I asked him to do with me what they had done with the Spanish player Calderé in Mexico. I pleaded with him. But nothing doing: they banned me for a year and a half, a year and a half for taking ephedrine without even knowing it. Ephedrine, the same thing that baseball players, basketball players, and football players in the United States take all the time. And we happened to be in the United States at the time. And the worst part is that I didn't even know I had taken it: I played with my soul, with my heart. Everyone in soccer knows that ephedrine doesn't help you run: everyone knows that!

I got to the World Cup clean as a whistle that year.

Because I knew it was my last chance to say to my daughters, "I'm a soccer player, and if you haven't seen what I'm capable of yet, I'm going to show you now." That's the only reason I celebrated the goal against Greece so loudly, so don't believe any of the bullshit that was said about me being high. I didn't need any drugs to return to the field or to let the world know the joy I was feeling! So if I cried and I am still crying today, it's because we were champions of the world and they stole our dream out from under us.

I remember it as if it were today, and my eyes fill with tears. Marcos Franchi came over, and from the look on his face you'd have thought someone died. And I was laughing for a change, having some fun with "El Vasco" Goycochea and his wife, Ana Laura. Claudia was there and so was my dad. Franchi said he had some bad news, but I had no idea what it could be. I had really trained for that World Cup! It was my comeback, my revenge. Franchi said that my anti-doping test after the game against Nigeria had come out positive. "Hon, we're going home," I said to Claudia, even before Marcos had finished explaining. He wanted me to know that management was discussing what to do, that they would do everything in their power. I didn't believe a word he said. Not a word. And I still don't believe it. Even today, I would like to get all the papers together, all the evidence, call up Dr. Peidró, who was the only one who knew what was up, and reopen the investigation.

By then, I no longer believed in anyone or in anything. It was the end of the world. That's why I went to my room and starting punching the wall, yelling and crying—and thinking about what was to come. What worried me the most was how my teammates were going to take it. We were in Boston, as happy as could be, and we had to fly to Dallas for the game against Bulgaria. It was torture to think of the next few hours. I remember all the media, all the people who were waiting when I got to Dallas . . . So much hope. And me wearing dark sunglasses because my eyes were red from crying and a dirty look on my face, a look that wasn't right for the captain of the team that had played better than any other team so far in that World Cup. The thing was, I knew everything and almost no one else did. It was torture, pure torture.

I swear that every time I tell the story, I get the same lump in my throat, like when I spoke afterward, in the interview they put on TV while my teammates were singing the national anthem. What I said that day was that they had cut off my legs. Because that's exactly how I felt. And Grondona, to name one guy, could have done more for me. He started out on the right foot but then he gave up on me. Deluca could have done more too. How about that, Eduardo Deluca, who's now facing jail time! "Deluca, do it for my daughters . . . ," I said to him. No one paid any attention. And they had plenty of arguments to defend me. I hadn't done cocaine, for Christ's sake, and it was the first time any of my tests had come back positive! Plus, I hadn't taken anything that would help me run faster.

I feel no more and no less guilty than I did at the time. I feel like someone made a mistake, but there was an explanation for it. We weren't halfway into the World Cup, but we were doing so well; we had such a great feeling that before the match against Bulgaria and after having beaten Greece and Nigeria, I felt like we were already in the finals. I know there was still a ways to go, but I felt like we had never been that close to winning it again, even though we had played two finals in the past three decades—World Cup '90 and World Cup 2014. When I say close, I mean in terms of how we were playing.

Then came France '98. I was long gone by then. It was the first time I watched the World Cup from the stands. That year, Passarella had a good team, a team with personality, but at a World Cup everything can change in just one play. I was there in Marseilles that afternoon in the game against the Netherlands. A long, long pass to Bergkamp—he was the only player who could have trapped it, plus he had Ayala and Chamot to back him up. Bergkamp brought the ball down with the tip of his toes and shot it past Roa and into the net. I think Argentina did well in that World Cup.

Now, in Japan 2002 the players were burned out before the games even started. With all due respect for Bielsa—because of everything "El Gringo" Heinze told me about him, because of the work I know he puts into it, because of the way he trains players, because I think he's a spectacular coach—I think he messed up there. He started training too early. Argentina was playing a fast game, and it focused on attacking instead of on having the ball—and that was a bad wager. Just like France, we were one of the favorites that year and we got eliminated at the group stage.

In Germany 2006, we had to focus on a fundamental play, which was when "El Pato" Abbondanzieri said he was injured and came out, and another goalie, Franco, was put in. I think the coach messed up there. Pékerman should have said to Pato, "You're staying in the whole game." Because then we could have put Messi in at any point and won the game. Let me explain: Ballack was exhausted; Germany was flagging and under a lot of pressure. They weren't going to be shooting on goal. Abbondanzieri must have had a reason to leave the game and, well, you can't blame a goalie for a team not winning the cup. But that play was critical. If the Argentines had made it to the quarterfinals, nothing would have stopped them.

MARADONA OR MESSI? MARADONA AND MESSI!

A lot of people ask me if Messi in 2006 was the Maradona of Spain '82. Maybe so. But if that was the case, then Messi 2010 would have to have been the Maradona of Mexico '86, and I can't sign off on that. Now, every World Cup is different, and, to win, a team always needs concentration and team spirit.

That's why, if I do decide to answer when I'm asked, "Maradona or Messi?" I say, "Maradona and Messi." Both were glorious players who wore the number 10 jersey; I had a great time, a lot of fun, so I've got no reason to envy Lio, who wears that jersey now. I always say that Riquelme was the best number 10, the best playmaker that Boca Juniors ever had, and Argentina's national team has had and continues to have players who know how to wear that jersey.

Messi could go to Russia in 2018 and win the World Cup. The only advice I'd give him is to train for it, all on his own.

Like I did with "El Profesor" Dal Monte before Mexico. That's what he has to do: get ready for the Russian World Cup all by himself. Because over at Barcelona he's taken care of, no problem; he's won what he had to win and could say now what I said to Napoli back in the day: "I love you guys a lot and I've given you my best, but now I need to focus on the national team." That way, he could go to Russia and bring home the cup. But he must be up to it mentally and physically—it will be his last chance. He doesn't have to start right now, but he would have to start four or five months from now.

I get him when he says he'd swap his five Ballon d'Or awards for just one World Cup. He's telling the truth, and he's right: all five of those don't add up to one World Cup.

And I'm not saying that out of envy. I won the Ballon d'Or only once, it's true—and it was an honorary award at that. I got mine in 1995 after I had come back to Argentina to play for Boca and the organizers—FIFA and *France Football* magazine—decided to change the rules, to make the award more universal, more global, more . . . serious. Until then, only Europeans won the Ballon d'Or. Just the same, two Argentines had managed to win it because they had played for European national teams. Two greats: Alfredo Di Stéfano, who got it in '57 and '59, and Enrique Omar Sívori, who got it in '61. Now, it never even crossed my mind to play for another national team, let alone assume a new nationality, though that way I could have won a few of them, right?

Thinking it over, if we want to play a little game, how many would I have won? Well . . . from '83 on, quite a few.

In '83, they gave it to that cold-hearted French player Platini. I had done some good things over at Barcelona; I had recovered from the hepatitis and "El Vasco" Goikoetxea still hadn't done me all that damage. I could have won it that year: that's one, take note.

And in '84, the Frenchman won it again. Come on, really? Let's say I might not have won it that year, since that was the year I left Barcelona, what with the big mess and after breaking my leg. All right, so by that year, let's say I still have just one.

In '85, Platini won it again. Really? What the hell, man, was he buying them? Okay, still just one for me that year.

Now in '86, Belanov won it. Igor Belanov? In '86? Come on! That was the year of the World Cup, with me playing for Argentina's national team, in case you forgot. That makes two Ballon d'Or awards.

And Gulli in '87? What about me, pops? Champion at Napoli! It was no mean feat turning Napoli into a champ, right after being champion of the world. So that makes three, three Ballon d'Or awards.

In '88, Marco van Basten? All right, he did win the UEFA Euro that year, but I had an even more amazing year. So that's four, four Ballon d'Or awards.

In '89, van Basten again? Over at Napoli, we won the UEFA Euro. That could have been my fifth.

In '90, my friend Matthäus? It's true, he won the World Cup playing for Germany. But I won the *scudetto* with Napoli and made it to the finals at the World Cup with Argentina. Ballon d'Or number six.

And in '91, the French player Jean-Pierre Papin? It sure must have been getting hard to find Europeans for the award, huh?

I'm not saying this to disrespect Messi in any way. What's more, I said great things about Messi before anyone else did. In 2005, they asked me about him, and this is what I said: "Messi's different. He's got a different playing style. He's tough, he's . . . it's not that the other players aren't tough, okay, but we've spent so much time looking for the next Maradona that we might have held some of our boys back. I mean, we held back boys who impressed us with their moves and filled our hearts, and then hit the ceiling. I feel like Messi is nowhere near his ceiling yet, you know what I mean? I feel like Messi is the player we've been waiting for." That's what I said: you can look it up—it's all there.

Just to clarify, Messi back then wasn't the Messi he is today. Now everyone says great things about Messi—no skin off their teeth. But way back then, I could tell he had something special. He had a unique way of handling the ball; he played at a different speed when he came up against the Europeans. He doesn't stop. That's why I say he likes the net more than I ever did. I was more focused on putting together plays than on scoring goals. I guess he is too, but I really liked helping the striker score. My eyes were on the whole field, his are on the net.

I think a few years from now, Lio will be an even more well-rounded player. Maybe he'll score fewer goals but his game will benefit. Now, there's a ceiling you hit, because you can't score three goals per game every game, but he'll make up for it by becoming a more well-rounded player. Because you may run a little slower with each passing year, but you gain experience to help avoid unnecessary friction. And you think things through a little more. You make only the wall passes you need to. He now shoots seventy wall passes a game but maybe in the future he'll shoot thirty and be a more well-rounded player, a player who comes back to midfield to get the ball, who takes free kicks, who switches play from one side of the field to the other.

What I have noticed is that the other team doesn't look scared when Lio takes a free kick. Boy, were they scared of me. When I took a free kick, the goalies would always be wondering if I was going to shoot on goal. But, in the one-on-one, Lio has a way with goalies: he's got the time and the mental speed to come in from one side, hook it past them, or shoot it over them. He does that better than anybody else.

The two of us are different, no two ways about it. In terms of personality mostly. Lio takes things a lot more calmly than I do. Mentally, when it comes to making decisions, Lio moves in slow motion. I was like a lightning bolt when it came to making decisions. I'm talking about personality now, and I'm saying this because I got to know Messi as a person and as a player. Maybe the difference is that he makes decisions a lot quicker on the field than off. Off the field, he does whatever the hell he wants, right? But, obviously, his life is a lot calmer than mine was.

I had to put together my own team, whereas Lio joined a powerhouse at Barcelona. Now, that's not his fault, just the opposite: he joined that team and makes a difference there.

I don't think Messi could do what I did at Napoli, though. Not because of talent, but because of personality. One thing I'm sure of: he has as much fun out there playing as I did. We're also different in terms of attitude. I was a rebel on and off the field. And I always say I did more damage to myself than to anyone else. But I also did whatever the hell I wanted to do. Lio is not a rebel off the field, but he does demand respect.

One thing I can say is that being team captain did him good. And just as a reminder: it wasn't Sabella or Bilardo who made him team captain. It was me. I made him captain because I could see how ticked he got when his teammates didn't pass to him at practice. That's his rebellion: convincing his teammates that they have to get the ball to him. From what I understand, he's a master on the PlayStation. At training camp, the boys play thirty games on the PlayStation and whoever wins sixteen is the best. On the field, Lio is a PlayStation player and his teammates understand that if they pass it to him he'll work things out. I don't see him as the kind of team leader who would demand to meet with Grondona the way I did, because that's just not who he is. If it came time to argue with someone like Grondona, someone other than Messi would go, but he would know exactly what was going on. And I have seen how he unleashes his fury on the field. One thing though: I don't think he loves winning as much as I do. I just don't think so . . .

I think it's stupid to compare us, and people who do are either anti-Maradona or anti-Messi. It's the folks who say that he's a Catalonian who doesn't know the words to the Argentine national anthem, the folks who say I'm a druggie. Though I do agree with a comparison that Arrigo Sacchi—a guy I adore—made. He was a major rival of mine when he was the coach at Milan and I was playing for Napoli, but he's a guy who really knows his stuff.

In *La Gazzetta dello Sport*, he wrote:

Maradona and Messi create a spectacle. Watching them play is thrilling, even for their rivals. Maradona interpreted soccer in a whole new way twenty or thirty years ago, making the game more about individual talent than about group trainings or a unified team. Maradona could always pull something out of his hat, making any team he played for special. Messi is a man of our times: he loves soccer and he plays with professionalism and enthusiasm. His enormous talent is less about instinct and more about years of soccer academies. He masterfully connects with his own team and strikes extraordinary chords with that splendid orchestra. Messi uses his team's synergy to gain advantages. Maradona was more autonomous, more self-sufficient. Unlike Diego, Lionel has no shortcomings, but maybe he hasn't fully developed his persona yet. Messi is more likely to follow the rules, more of a professional and less of a showman. But both love soccer, each in his own way. Each is a player of his times who will leave an unforgettable mark as an all-time great in the history of the sport.

I agree with that 100 percent. Messi and I are different from one another and from everyone else. Alejandro Dolina, a radio host who I think the world of, once said something that really hit home. In a TV interview, Dolina was talking about Messi, saying all the wonderful things that should be said about him. Half an hour later and all of a sudden Alejandro Fantino, the guy doing the interview, said to him, "And what about Maradona?"

"Oh, Maradona is a whole different story . . . Listen, Messi has been playing for years, right? Well, I had to watch Messi for a whole year before I realized he's the best in the world. With Diego, seeing one play was enough."

I loved that. Dolina is a real soccer fan. Now, he's better at talking about soccer than at playing it, because once we had ourselves a little pickup game in Punta del Este, and Dolina is still trying to stop the ball.

BRINGING THE WORLD CUP HOME AGAIN

Before the World Cup in Brazil, I said that Messi didn't have to win to be the best player in the world. He was already the best player, and he still is. I mean, let's not mistake salt for sugar—one thing's got nothing to do with the other. Winning the World Cup would have been fantastic for Argentina, fantastic for the fans and for Lio. But whether he wins the World Cup has no bearing on everything he's done to get where he is today; no one can question that. And he's up there with the greatest players in history, the ones everyone names: Di Stéfano, Pelé, Cruyff, and me . . . And him. Three Argentines. Three! That's what we need to remember.

Each of them stood out in his day; each one dared to snatch someone else's throne. Some, like Messi, had a one-on-one with a player like Cristiano Ronaldo. In our day, there was a lot of competition, what with Rummenigge, Zico, Platini. You had to compete with all kinds of players to be considered the best.

And I would add some other guys to that list, guys from different periods. Rivellino, my idol, of course. What a superb player—he came to *De Zurda* to talk with me during the last World Cup. And then there's Rummenigge, Romário, Ronaldo, Ronaldinho, Del Piero, Rivaldo, and Totti.

I admit it, a lot of times I get choked up thinking about them. It's overpowering. I love them. I really feel something for these guys; it's my weak spot.

But that's not how I feel about Pelé—and it goes beyond soccer. I barely ever saw him play, but the fact that he sided with management, not with the players, is a disgrace. I won't forgive him for that, and that's a huge difference between him and me. He should have recognized that his teammates made him great: not a single manager helped make Pelé what he was. But he forgot that.

But all that's history, and I want to talk some about the future too. And so I ask myself, what do we have to do to be world champions again?

And I've got the answer: what we need more than anything else to be world champions again is for AFA to become a serious soccer organization. Put an end to the nepotism. And put an end to saying that because so-and-so won, there's automatically a spot for him in the organization. If so-and-so won, he should be there, sure, but only if he won through hard work. Only if he won because he had a plan. And that's the thing with AFA today, no one's got a plan.

I would say to the guys running AFA, now that it's not AFA anymore. They've torn AFA into so many pieces that there's nothing left. If thirty-eight plus thirty-eight is seventy-five votes, we're in really bad shape! What happened at the AFA elections made world news—it was a total embarrassment.

We're fighting over power and money instead of concentrating on what needs to be done for Argentina to bring the World Cup home again.

And that really pisses me off. Plus, as a country, we need to get back to our roots. And those roots say that the big teams support the little teams. And now you watch the Argentine league games on TV and see the visitor section is empty, because visiting fans were banned back in 2013, and it looks like a game of bachelors versus married men in someone's backyard. That's what I'm talking about when I say support. The quality of the Argentine leagues has gone way down in terms of how the game is played and how much fun it is to watch.

And I've got to say that everything that happens at AFA— and in FIFA—has been Grondonafied. Grondona, Blatter, and Platini are all cut from the same cloth. There's no doubt in my mind that if he hadn't bit the dust beforehand, the first guy Interpol would have arrested would have been Julio Humberto Grondona. The very first guy on their list.

Blatter was who he was because of Grondona. And in the thirty years since we brought a World Cup home all they've done is throw us a few bones with the U-20s, letting us win a few of those. It's been thirty years, boys. Thirty years! All those years Grondona was over at FIFA, we didn't bring the cup home once.

But now Grondona's gone. And we've got to start all over again. The recruiter for the seniors has to visit the U-15s. Enough of some coaches playing with three on defense and others playing with four on defense. Enough experimenting. Enough.

I'd do what the Germans do. Put something together where you start working with the kids and help them work their way up. How come our boys get to the first division without ever learning how to kick the ball properly? That's not acceptable. It's not acceptable that we don't produce any good fullbacks or midfielders. Changing that would be a step in the right direction.

Or what the English did about the hooligans to put an end to the violence. Hooligans would go in and tear the stadium apart. You couldn't sit next to someone wearing the other team's jersey because he'd break your head open with a beer bottle. And now it's a pleasure to sit and watch a Premier game—I catch one whenever I'm in England, or on television when I'm in Dubai.

THE STYLE OF ARGENTINE SOCCER

I'm not saying we need to copy anyone. But we've got to find what works and adapt it to Argentine soccer, to what Argentine soccer needs.

And, of course, Argentine soccer has a style all its own. We need to recover that style. I'd define it as the Menotti style. I mean, it was in '74, when "El Flaco" Menotti started training the players for the '78 World Cup, that we really started to compete against the heavyweights. The national team should be our number-one priority. And our players should grow up at home and train here.

At one point, I was under a contract with a no-trade clause, and though it pissed me off at the time, now I realize why it was there. If I let my grandson Benjamín play today, I'd have twenty-five agents at the door of my daughter's house ready to whisk him away or sign him on. Come on, let's get serious! Nowadays a player like Calleri has to goal his way through Termas de Río Hondo to be sold to Inter, which then lends him to Bologna, only to end up playing for São Paulo. They're out of their minds. What are they trying to come up with? No need to reinvent the wheel, right?

That's why we have to fix this from the bottom up. What we have to do is agree on a serious plan for our young players, the ones who we've lost to other countries. We need to make it a priority not to let those kids leave until they're sixteen or seventeen. There are Argentine players other countries want to nationalize because they've never played for our national team. Sure, those are kids who left Argentina at the age of twelve— they don't have that sense of patriotism. They shouldn't leave until they've at least formed a memory of the Argentine jersey.

That's just for starters. And something else: if a player has an agent before he's seventeen, he shouldn't be allowed to play for his national team. Parents—not agents—have to bring up their children, not the other way around.

So there should be no looking for saviors—not in family or in sport. And that's my final word. Because, to bring things to a close, I'd like to ask a final heartfelt question, a question all of us have to ask if we want Argentine soccer to get better, if we want another world championship, if we don't want to let another thirty years go by before bringing the World Cup home again: what comes after Messi?